Make Money In MLM

Full time, Part time, Anytime for a Lifetime

Bob Powers, MR. MLM

Life Long Publishing
An International Sales Wellness Publishing Company
PO Box 34352, Charlotte NC 28234, USA
www.LifeLongPublishing.com

Library of Congress Control Number
00-131114

© Powers, Robert M.
Make Money in MLM: full time, part time, anytime for a lifetime.

ISBN 0-9673451-0-3
1. Business. 2. Sales.

Printed in the United States of America
10 9 8 7 6 5 4 3 2

Acknowledgments

Thanks to all the distributors who have shared their stories of struggle and success. It is you; in search of a superior life, that has made this industry great.

Thanks to the speakers, teachers and motivators who have kept a candle of enthusiasm burning brightly for their business support teams to follow—and for the great example, you have set.
In you, we have truly found a better way to live.

What would you pay for one good idea that could revolutionize your business and skyrocket your dreams?
(Price on back cover)

Table of Contents

Introduction

Why MLM?
Independent Business Ownership (IBO), Entrepreneurship, Multi-level Marketing (MLM), Small Business, Sales, Network Marketing, Referral Merchandising, Interactive Distribution™, Neighborhood Networking, Multiplication Marketing, Duplication Distribution...the name you call it doesn't really matter, what we are talking about here is you making a percentage of the efforts of numerous people. If a certain name or word offends you, simply replace it for one that works for you and your organization. We refer to it here as MLM for the sake of ease.

We are going to assume for the sake of argument that you are considering becoming a distributor in an MLM, or you already are one. We won't spend precious time and energy here sorting through what it is to be a distributor, who would most benefit from being one, or the why behind your involvement. Many wonderful books have addressed those very topics and you will find my favorites in the recommended reading section at the back of this book.
Let us assume you are very clear about your personal reasons, you have already set your goals, and you are simply looking to take your business to the next level.

If this book belongs to you, read it with a highlighter or pen so you can quickly reference ideas that jump out at you. When you go back to implement these ideas, they will be readily available and easy to locate.
If you have questions regarding content in this book, or you would like me to personally come to your next business opportunity meeting to share with your group the latest techniques relating to MLM's, you can contact me through my website at www.Mr.MLM.net

Chapter 1:

Why Reinvent the Wheel?

Over the years, multilevel empires have been built with a variety of tactics that still work today. And while there is virtue in saying "Don't reinvent the wheel, do what has worked in the past..." it is important to acknowledge times are changing. As we aggressively market in this new millennium, it is crucial to realize the information age will change the way we do business, the way we handle customers, the way we order and ship products, the way we meet and recruit distributor's and how we keep in touch with them.

I guess it is fair to say the old way still works, and the new way works too – the difference however, is the difference between riding a bicycle and driving a car. The new way is so much faster, more efficient, and cost effective than the old way of downline distribution.

So join me on an unconventional joy ride through the past into the future and together we will explore what has worked, why it has worked, and how you might continue making money in your venture today and tomorrow.

I have compiled thirty four years of business experience in referral marketing, networking, marketing, consulting, selling and people skills, along with the best ideas I've learned from this era's top multilevel millionaires to show you an easy and effortless way to produce the income you've always dreamed about.

Is This Company is Right for Me?

Any time you begin a new venture, questions naturally pop up in your mind. You want to make sure you are making the right choice because you don't want to look like a fool to your family and friends if it doesn't work out. Here are some basic guidelines to take the pinch out of a new business decision.

Company Research

The opportunity behind any new or unfamiliar business enterprise should be thoroughly researched. If you were applying for a new job you would pull most likely pull up the company's website, read their annual reports, drive by their location and meet some of the happily employed people before committing away your future there. The same rules apply to less traditional business.

- Check the financials of the company before you make an investment.

- See if they are members in good standing with the Direct Selling Association.

- You can request an audited financial statement or annual report to determine if you are in agreement with their accounting procedures.

- If any complaints have been filed against the company, it should be listed with your state attorney general or your local Better

Business Bureau. If it is a fraudulent complaint, it will most likely be listed with the National Fraud Information Center.

- And then remember if you take a job with a traditional company that has a great pay plan, bonuses, incentives, paid vacations, sick leave, and so on, but you never show up for work, you don't get any of the benefits offered.

The same rules apply as a distributor. If you agree to a compensation plan but you do not work the business, do not blame the company for your failure.

Compensation

Are you paid primarily on products sold in your company or from your sponsoring efforts? Some state laws require 70% of the customer's sales be generated from people outside your business team. This prevents you buying products and then downloading them to your organization, filling their garages and attics with products, they may never sell.

To prevent the illusion of illegal schemes, many companies now have a direct order program where you order products as you consume them, and they are typically products you would normally buy anyway. You simply earn credit when you or the distributors in your group order.

My Investment

- What are the costs of getting involved?
- Is there an up front investment?
- Will you need a business start-up kit?
- Is there a refund on unsold inventory if you choose not to sell your products within the first 30 days?

- Are you serious about working the business?

Remember if you treat your business like a hobby, it may be fun and exciting but it will never pay you like a business. Hobbies cost money not earn money. Business, treated and worked like a business will reap you the financial rewards that will lead you down the road to financial freedom.

Earnings

Realize in any company, traditional or otherwise, there are a few people making all the money. All the rest of the people are making okay or marginal to no money. Moreover, it doesn't have any thing to do with getting in on the ground floor.

There is a spooky myth that all the ground floor/start up people make all the money. And while this is a wonderful way to shift the blame if you don't make it in the business, consider this: if you take some-one with a strong work ethic and you give them a new opportunity, they will make a success of themselves. Similarly, if you take a per-son who lacks work ethic and you strategically place them in a pro-ductive environment they will still be lazy and you both lose. It is the person, who makes the money in business, not a position.

Mentoring

Every success coach today suggests if you want to be great, then walk and talk with those who are great. Slash your learning curve by observing those who have already done what you want to do. If you were to buy a franchise, you would go to franchise school and for a small fortune, you would learn the success rules of how to run a franchise. They would teach you to do what other franchise owners have learned by trial and error.

So instead of going to franchise or small business school, put yourself on a mission to find a mentor or many mentors who have mastered what you want to do.

Find somebody who is fabulous at networking and make them your mentor for networking. Find a mentor who excels in time management and have them teach you how to maximize your day for ultimate productivity.
Find a health coach who can get you on a good exercise program and energy diet that will improve your physical well being and self-confidence.
Find a marketing guru and hang out with them as much as possible. Learn to think like they think and sell like they sell.
Find a teenage mentor who knows their way around the World Wide Web and the Internet and have them teach you how to navigate your way to electronic success.

Don't limit yourself to just one mentor. Find many mentors who specialize in various aspects of your small business. And don't be so egotistical that you can't ask for help until you find the "Perfect Mentor" such a person doesn't exist. All you have to do is find somebody who knows more than you do, and then seek to learn and apply all they know.

Realize too, there is a difference between a mentor and a cheer-leader. Your mentor is not necessarily your cheerleader. Though he or she may encourage you, their point is not to pump you up, but to confirm what you are doing right and honestly help you correct areas that need improvement.

Be grateful for any time a mentor might spend with you. Mentors are real people too with life's demands of housekeeping, errands to run businesses to operate, telephone calls and emails to return. Don't suck away all their precious energy just because you need help.

The rule of thumb is to ask for help.

- When you get advice or information, apply what you have learned.
- Tweak what you have applied to see if there is a faster, more economical, more logical way to do what you have implemented.
- Go back to your mentor with your findings.
- Allow them to help you tweak the process until you have mastered what you sought to learn.

If you are meeting with a mentor, email or fax them your agenda in advance so they can prepare to meet with you. This tells your mentor you are serious about his or her help. It also shows your level of preparation and the fact that you are respectful of their time.

Show up when you say you will be there and be teachable. Don't act as if you already know what they are telling you. If you do know, that is just a confirmation to you that you are on the right track. Still thank them for their help.

It is easy to find mentors who will give you free help. Some do charge for their expertise and that is fine too. You may want to seek out free help in the beginning until you have learned all you can and then solicit professional help for areas that you are stumped on, or want additional training. If you need professional help and cannot afford it in the beginning, consider bartering for products you sell or services that you yourself might offer. Some mentors will give you advice in exchange for lunch or dinner. Don't rule out any possibility.

Some professional help that is directly related to your business can be tax deducted and therefore can easily be budgeted for. A good mentor can save you hundreds of hours of your own trial and error, which often makes them more cost effective for your business than trying to learn it all yourself.

Prepare yourself today while learning the ropes of independent business ownership to be a mentor one-day. Consider it a compliment the day someone calls you up to ask questions about how you got started, and never be too busy to share with them what someone once shared with you.

Success Reminders

- The old way of marketing still works, and the new way works too – the difference however, is the difference between riding a bicycle and driving a car.

- Take someone with a strong work ethic and give them a new opportunity, and watch them make a success of themselves. Take a person who lacks work ethic and give them the same opportunity and you are wasting your time.

- Remember it is natural to have questions and feelings of insecurity when you begin a new venture.

- Research and check out the company just as you would a traditional business.

- Determine in advance, how you will be paid, how often you will be paid, and what you have to do in order to get paid.

- Remember if you treat your business like a hobby, it may be fun and exciting but it will never pay you like a business. Hobbies cost money not earn money. Treating a business like a business will allow you to reap the rewards of financial freedom.

- It is quite irresponsible to blame someone else or the company you are representing for your lack of effort.

- Be flexible and if you see a technique that you are using doesn't work, give yourself permission to try something else.

- Don't be so egotistical that you can't ask for help until you find the "Perfect Mentor" such a person does not exist.

- If you are meeting with a mentor, send them your agenda in advance so they can prepare.

- Show up on time, prepared to learn.

- A mentor is not a cheerleader they are there to help you determine what corrective action needs to be taken.

- Prepare yourself today while learning the ropes of independent business ownership to be a mentor one-day.

Chapter 2:

Your Biggest Asset...YOU!

Business Ownership

In any business, it is easy to want control so you can determine the outcome of your success. And while you do have control over which company you choose to align yourself with, chances are you don't have control over that company's inventory, production procedures, shipping deadlines, ordering, fulfillment and so on.

If you are joining an existing marketing company, chances are you are sliding into a program with an existing pay plan already in place. This is great for you, since many problems and glitches that haunt start up businesses have already have been resolved.

Now that the fundamentals are out of the way let us focus on what you do have control over. You.

Realize as you involve yourself with any company that your biggest asset going in—and coming out, is you.

> "The difference between happy and productive people and the people who are not,
> is found in what they do and how they think."
> - Jim Cathcart

You are bringing to the business all of the business experience you have had up until' now. You will be drawing from years (or lack of) of networking involvement. If you have disciplined business habits, you will most likely use them as a distributor too. Likewise if you have less than desirable work habits, and you are a big procrastinator and you hate using the telephone to follow up with distributors and prospects, it is suspect you will repeat those same behaviors in this business as well. Unless...you make a commitment to yourself, your family, and your future that, you are going to learn new techniques and change.

> *"Insanity is doing the same things*
> *Over and over again*
> *While hoping for new results."*

In typical corporate business, there is a lot of mudslinging between co-workers (here it would be distributors), gossip, slandering, unlucky moments, and decisions made without your suggestion. It is crucial to remember that it is part of real business. Don't let it bog you down. Even the biggest corporations with the best game plans against slander, experience a blow every once in a while.

You do have control over your own attitude and how you feel about the business, you have chosen. Realize also, that anybody you sponsor into this business, will watch you, and reflect your attitudes and opinions.

So if you are having a bad day, spend some quiet time listening to motivational tapes and reading good books and working on getting your attitude back, and if you have a fabulous day, go sponsor the world.

You also have control over how you look, how you feel, how much energy and time you invest into your business. So focus on the things you can control and I promise you will get out of your business, exactly what you put into it.

Be the kind of person you are looking to sponsor. Ask yourself:

1. *Would you sponsor you?*
2. *Are you gregarious and outgoing?*
3. *Do you have strong business skills? If not, are you willing to learn some?*
4. *Are you a great listener?*
5. *Do you understand people?*
6. *Are you motivator?*
7. *Are you an enthusiast?*
8. *If not, you might reconsider this business, or take a course to improve your interpersonal skills.*

In the future pages together we will cover lots of stuff about where to find prospects, how to network with them and what to say when you sponsor them. We will discuss marketing over the Internet through newsletters and advertisements, but when all is said and done, your success in this business comes down to three things:
1. People
2. People
3. People

You are now in the people business. Without people, your business is nothing. If you are anti-social and you do not like people, you had better keep your job. Your attempts as an independent business owner will be futile.

What if You Don't Know Anyone?

Make a point right now, that starting today you will go out and meet one new person—every day for the rest of your life. And when I say meet one new person, I mean learn about them, their likes and dislikes, and exchange enough information that you can stay in touch with them either by telephone or email for the rest of your life.

If you meet more than one, good for you – you are ahead of most of the rest of the population living in their comfort zones. So make sure you get out of the house every single day to meet somebody you do not already know. Then add them to your Rolodex of people to remember.

Your sales and social pipeline will never dry up if you keep involved in meeting new people every day.
And once you have earned the right to call a person friend, they will give you more referrals than you could ever hope to sponsor.

Yin and Yang

The yin and yang philosophy is penetrating our western culture. The Tai Chi symbol itself was designed to represent that life is in constant motion. The yin or even energy blends with the yang or uneven energy creating a wheel. You will notice that in the yang, there is a small circle of yin, and in the yin there is a small circle of yang. That small circle reminds us that even in good times, there is a bit of bad, and in bad times there is a bit of good. In dark times, there is a bit of light, and in light times, there is a bit of dark. We must have a touch of sadness to appreciate happiness and a touch of happiness in sad times to give us hope.

This applies to us in business to remind us that all days are not wonderful, nor are all days bad. Just as the wheel of life turns, so does the wheel of business.

If you are on the upside today, the wheel will eventually turn by the law of nature, and you will be on the downside. Prepare and plan your activities appropriately so you can get maximum amount of return for your energy and emotion.

And if you are on a downward slope, the wheel of life will turn again and soon you will be on top. Don't get arrogant when times are up and don't get cross when times are down. Realize there is a bit of up in down, and a bit of down in up.

Remembering the Tai Chi helps us keep all things in perspective.

Your attitude is easier to control if you know in which direction you are headed. It takes some of the guess work and stress out of living every day.

In order to keep your spirits up, your energy high and your attitude bright, learn to balance the wheel of life through organization.

Organization in Minutes

If you were to trace the lives of successful people, you would find one common behavior repeatedly...that is the ability to organize and prioritize daily activities.

Successful people view their time and energy as resources, and they invest them wisely in order to gain a maximum return.

> *"I've never met a poor person who was consciously aware of time."*
> *- Bill Gouldd*

Time Management Made Easy

Learn to get up a few minutes before dawn and make a list of "TO Do's." Then make a conscious decision to address each item on your list and either:

1. Complete it
2. Outsource it
3. Eliminate it

One of the biggest mistakes small business people make is disorganization and lack of concentration. Instead of using their time to their advantage, they piddle it away doing nothing in particular. Getting drinks, eating, watching the news, checking the stock market on the Internet, checking to see if they have any emails. Calling their family and friends, reading their mail, doing laundry, and going to the grocery store and a whole list of other things to menial to mention.

Some people even consider this unproductive time "Getting ready time" They are getting ready to do the business. And no money was ever made during that getting ready to get ready time.

> *"If you always do what you've always done,*
> *You'll always be what you've always been."*
> *- Dexter Yager*

The best part of independent business ownership (and the allure to most people getting involved) is the freedom to be their own boss. You get to do what you really love and work with the people you want to work with. You get to set your own deadlines and reap the rewards of your own success - or failure.

And don't forget that everything is a trade off. Everything.
If you choose to spend your day idly chatting with friends who are going nowhere in life, then you're in good company because that is exactly where you're headed. And by the same token, if you choose to get out in the marketplace and make something happen, you will soon find that every key on your ring opens wide the doorways of opportunity, prosperity and freedom.

Of course, it is easy to become overwhelmed by all there is to do as a distributor. And overwhelm is accompanied by stress. In order to avoid stress; learn to allocate your time properly.

> *"Avoid the trap of an unplanned day."*

- Schedule meetings and coffee appointments to particular days of the week.

- Schedule deliveries and running errands to a certain day and then every week on the same day run those errands so you don't get distracted by picking up mail, laundry or groceries when you should be out prospecting.

- Schedule sales calls and prospecting to particular days of the week.

- Use the days you are not seeking new business to follow up with existing prospects and distributors and to do three way calls, return calls and postcards.

- Pick an uninterrupted off-hour to read and respond to your email and telephone calls. Pick the same hour each day. This will create an expectation from your family that you are "working" during this hour and must not be interrupted.

- Schedule a research hour. Pick an hour a day to read late breaking information from newsmagazines, industry books, websites, and so on. While you may have a good grasp of what is transpiring in your industry today, it is guaranteed to change. Remember this is the information age and business is changing at an incredible speed.

- Put a deadline on your projects so you have a finish time to shoot for.

The Importance of a Weekly Review

In corporate jobs, it is typical to have a weekly review with your boss to determine the needs of your job for that week. Often you report what you have done so far and together you determine what you will need in order to complete the unfinished tasks at hand.

This kind of routine also works for independent business ownership. Plan early Monday morning a meeting with yourself or your mentor and determine your objectives for the week.

Make a game plan based on your progress of last week. This is where you analyze what you did right and what needs improvement. This is a truth session where you review your dreams and goals and see how far along you are on the path of success. Take notes just and jot down ideas that arise during your brainstorm.

Take your days off in advance so you know when you will be working and when you have time to play. One of the biggest mistakes small business people make is they forget to take time off, and then they always feel like they are working. This kind of thinking and acting is far from practical and the result is constantly working but never getting much done because there is no "down time".

> *"The man who is always killing time*
> *Is really killing his own chances in life*
> *While the man who is destined for success*
> *Is the man who makes time live*
> *by making it useful."*
> *-Arthur Brisbane*

Give yourself permission to relax and take time off and then you won't feel guilty when you do.

No More "no show" Appointments

It is common while out prospecting to show up for an appointment only to find a "no show" meaning the person you were planning to meet never showed up.

Common courtesy suggests that you wait ten to fifteen minutes for your prospect to arrive. If they don't show up, leave a diplomatic note that suggests your disappointment but allows them to keep their dignity (in case they want to reschedule with you.) Such a note might read:

> "Hey Eric,
> Sorry I missed you. I hope you were not in an accident or anything. Anyway, I had another appointment so I had to eventually leave. Call me and let me know you are okay and we will reschedule our meeting.

Cheers!
Melanie Williams
704-123-4567

If you were meeting at a public meeting place you can email the note or drop a postcard with the same message.

If you are a time conservationist you will find these are great tricks to keep you focused and on schedule in the networking business.

Time Tricks to Keep You Focused

One of my favorites is to meet people at a coffeehouse. There are actually several reasons why. They are:

1. If we meet for coffee instead of lunch, then I can determine within five or ten minutes if we have compatible goals and can work together. This I have determined in a few minutes not an hour or two.

2. If we are unable to do business together, we have invested ten minutes of our day, a cup of coffee, and we are on our way, we are not obligated to sit through the rest of a lunch or dinner.

3. Coffee (if I am buying) is less expensive than lunch and duplicable. My prospects are more likely to duplicate a coffee appointment in the beginning than an extravagant lunch with a prospect or a ritzy diner.

4. A coffeehouse is a fun environment that is conducive to business and wait staff asking if we need more drinks or desert will not interrupt us.

5. A coffeehouse is not my office or yours. If we are in my office, I have a tendency to get off track with incoming telephone calls or the UPS man who needs a signature for a delivery. Your house or office invites similar distractions for you.

6. A coffeehouse is a great place to rotate business. Suppose you are meeting with Bill who is a prospect who listens eagerly to your presentation, when Amy enters to be your next appointment.

Suddenly Bill meets Amy and realizes you are smoothly running your business out of a coffee shop, and he understands how easy that is and sees himself duplicating his business the same way.
Amy meeting Bill sees you are running your business out of a coffee shop and she understands how easy that is and she thinks she could do that too.
Then you start your presentation all over again, (only you invite Bill to stay and listen, although he just heard your presentation, you are now training him how to be a distributor.)
After half an hour Karen walks in and sees that you are in the process of a meeting and realizes that you are running your business out of a coffee shop and she knows how easy that is, she can do that...and the cycle continues. (This time you invite Bill and Amy to stay and listen.)

7. One of my favorite uses of a coffeehouse is to gather together all of your distributors who want to be in the business but aren't motivated enough to work the plan.
You know the ones, they all want your attention and they all want your expertise and your help. They want you to hold their hand and do the business for them, so they can make money without putting too much effort in themselves. They don't want to make any telephone calls and they are too busy to come to weekly business oppor-

tunity meetings. So you announce you are having a coffee chat and tell them where and when to meet.

Instead of spending precious time and energy individually coercing them to do the business, you simply group them all together in one big happy coffee chat. This way you can lead a group discussion about changes in the business and offer group help.

- Make sure your friends and distributors know when the coffee chat begins and ends so they learn to duplicate those same behaviors. (And then leave when you said you were finished. Hanging out all day with them subconsciously eats away your credibility.)

Can You Meet Me Tomorrow?

Another secret of those who are prosperous is when they set appointments they put a cap on their time. Instead of having a meeting and then just hanging out the rest of the day, they officially end the appointment and return to their business.

Can I meet you tomorrow at ten? Is a fine question to ask, but also mention; I am free then until eleven. This lets your prospects know that you respect your time and they need to follow by the same rules.
When you are working from a schedule you will find that you are more punctual and so is your distributor. They know your schedule will continue with or without them therefore they show you respect by showing up on time.

How to End Procrastination

Successful people in business and in life do not just indecisively put things off. They strategically accomplish their goals one at a time, on purpose. They know procrastination and unfinished projects create imbalance and stress.

Part of prioritizing and time conservation is doing what you love to do and either getting good at the stuff you hate, or finding somebody else to do it for you.

Ignoring necessary elements of business are not the stepping stones to your success; they will simply be the boulders that get in your way.

> *"Procrastination is a learned behavior*
> *That can be unlearned by action."*
> *– Bob Powers*

Learn to stretch and get out of your comfort zone and address the stuff you have been putting off. You will notice that it not only clears your conscience, but it frees up a good deal of energy and worry.

The Trap of Over Commitment

Independent business champions learn by organization and execution what their individual capabilities are, and they learn when enough is enough. They learn not to take on too many projects and they learn that it is okay to say, "no, thanks though for considering me" when they have reached their personal limit of obligations and commitments.

It is really easy to get sucked into community involvement with neighborhood block parties, chambers of commerce meetings, leads clubs, volunteer work and so on. And while those may be great places to network, it is important to remember, at least in the beginning that none of those groups pay your bills. If you just network and never follow the other crucial steps of follow-up, you might wind up being the most popular and broke person on your street.

You Can't Have It All

Successful people know that you cannot have it all, and they learn to set realistic (large, but attainable) goals. They realize that you cannot own the world, and would not want the responsibility that comes along with it, if you could.

They begin where they are, with whatever equipment or lack of it they have, and they make the most of their time and their lives by being wise stewards. And as they invest their resources in the future and in people, they become the shareholders of success.

> *"He is rich or poor according to what he is, not what he has."*
> *– Henry Ward Beecher*

Keeping Up With the Jones's

In the beginning, before your money begins rolling in realize that it is not necessary to keep up with the Jones's. As you do your dream building and set goals to obtain fun stuff from business profits, make certain you are buying things because you really want or need them, not just because you bought them on sale or the neighbors have them.

For years there has been a theme in network marketing of "Fake it, till you make it" meaning you buy things beyond your means to give the illusion that you are very successful in the business—so others will want what you have, and will join you in business.

And while new cars and new houses and boats are great fun, there is wisdom in waiting until you can afford them instead of amassing great debt.

> *"The things that mean the most in life, money cannot buy."*

Why do we care anyway what others think of us?
Is it because we want others to like us and approve of us? That is the whole philosophy behind "keeping up with the Jones's. We continue to work long hours to have money to buy things we think we need. And often those same things end up being donated to charitable organizations or yard sales because not only did we not need those things we bought, but we didn't want them either.
Somewhere along the way we bought into an image that an object would or could bring happiness.

So ask yourself each time you are about to purchase something, ask yourself "Will I really use this item, or will it someday end up in a yard sale?"

If it is an item exclusively intended to impress others, give yourself permission not to purchase it.
Learn to live within your means. And as you earn a significant income, hopefully you will become a significant individual, and will instinctively know how to invest your money on things that matter and will help other people.

Success Reminders

- Realize as you involve yourself with any company that your biggest asset going in—and coming out, is you.

- Things that are measured tend to improve.

- He is rich or poor according to what he is, not what he has.

- Your sales and social pipeline will never dry up if you keep involved in meeting new people every day.

- Procrastination and unfinished projects create imbalance and stress.

- The wheel of life continually turns. Prepare and plan your activities appropriately so you can get maximum amount of return for your energy and emotion through it's turning.

- Successful people view their time and energy as resources and they invest them wisely in order to gain a maximum return.

- When scheduling an appointment, also schedule when it will conclude.

- Part of prioritizing and time conservation is doing what you love to do and either getting good at the stuff you hate, or finding somebody else to do it for you.

- Plan your vacations and time off in advance to avoid guilt from not working.

Chapter 3:

First Impressions

Who you are, the ways you dress, the way you carry yourself, are all advertisements for your business.
Subconsciously people make a decision about your professionalism and how well put together you are based on the impression you leave. Make sure if you are representing a company, either your own or someone else's, that you look the part. You don't have to wear expensive clothing, but do make sure it fits and is clean and pressed.

If you don't know how to iron, learn.
If you do not own an iron, make it one of your first purchases.
Wal-Mart, Kmart and Target all sell irons and ironing boards for about as little money as it will cost you for dinner. Being pressed is the difference between looking like a hundredaire and a millionaire.

Even your casual clothing can look top notch instead of looking like it's been sitting at the bottom of your hamper for a week.
If you own clothing that has permanent wrinkles, try using a little spray starch. When using starch, spray your clothes and let it set never iron starch on your clothing when the starch is wet or it will flake on you. Starching your clothes will bring the crispness back to life in just about any article of clothing. When the clothes you are wearing no longer represent you, discard or recycle them.

What is Professional Attire?

Even if your clothing isn't exactly the latest fashion, most anything goes now. Being comfortable about your looks will make you seem more self-confident.

Wear only clothes that represent you and the message you are trying to convey.
Untucked shirts send a sloppy leisure message - that you don't give a hoot about your personal appearance. If you are casual still be well groomed and organized in your looks.

> *"Distractions in clothing*
> *take away from personal power."*

Baby-sit Kids Not Clothing

It is not fashionable to fidget with your clothes under any circumstances.

- Get rid of all the skirts that ride up your thigh when you sit down.

- Toss your shirts that are missing buttons or sew new ones on.

- Pin shoulder pads in place so they do not slip around, or remove them all together.

- Give away shoes that hurt your feet, especially if you spend a good deal of your time walking around or standing during your networking.

- If the zipper is broken in your pants, take them to a tailor or buy new pants. Hoping no one will notice is just fancy hoping.

- Match your clothing and accessories to your personality and skin type.

Mix-N-Match

If you are color blind, have someone go shopping with you to determine the clothes that work for your skin tone.

Pick four basic colors that work for you and buy all of your clothes and accessories in those colors. You will be able to mix-n-match outfits in your closet on days when there's nothing to wear, and your shoes and accessories will also be interchangeable. When you go shopping, you will save time not sorting through clothing racks that are not one of "your colors".

The Do's and Don'ts of Accessories

Noisy costume jewelry is fun to wear and as a society we've dedicated a whole day in October to wear it - but the general rule is if it takes away from your natural looks, you've probably over done it. I recently sat in a meeting watching a beautiful woman speak. She had a wonderful face and bright eyes, but her three inch silver earrings kept shouting for attention. I am sure she said important things, but her dancing earbobs stole the show.

Accessories are intended to enhance your natural beauty, not cover it. Remember that in the accessory game anything that is not "natural" becomes an accessory.

If you have a sculptured hair do, your do itself is considered an accessory. Or if you wear your hair in a long braid, that braid is an accessory. Designer or unusual buttons are accessories as is custom stitching or monograms on garments. Those glittery glues and crafty blouses women wear with beads and stars attached are accessories and should be worn with taste.

Eye glasses, wrist watches, ring watches, pins, scarves, hats, purses, wallets, day-timers, neckties, fingernails and fingernail polishes, ornaments on clothing or shoes, and pantyhose with designs, are all accessories aside from usual rings, necklaces earrings and bracelets.
Take care not to over do it, you do not want to look like a walking window display.

Often, less is more when it comes to accessories. Personal power is not derived from clanky trinketry.

> *"Be conservative, Be tasteful and never show all you have."*
> *-   Glenna Salisbury*

The big misnomer in independent marketing is that you have to flash your gaudy jewelry at people. Originally, this was intended to create a visual that you were really making it in the business, but over time, it has been realized that conservative jewelry also shows class without alienating your prospect. Be certain that all of your clothing, jewelry and accessories are worn with taste.

Simplicity Sells
If it has been a while since someone complimented you on your smile, you might consider de-accessorizing.

> *"A winning smile makes winners of us all."*

Makeup is another form of design wear and often part of a woman's daily routine. And while I am not encouraging an "earthy looking" revolution, let us remember the purpose of makeup is to brighten your natural beauty, not hide it. The ugliest woman will be far better off with a healthy glow and smile than with chisel-proof foundation and blush.

And women have enough class to apply your makeup in the necessary room, not in public places like business opportunity meetings and restaurants. You wouldn't think of putting on your deodorant in public, so don't put perfume or lipstick on in public either. Combing your hair in public is just like brushing your teeth in public - another unclassy move.

Top 10 Unclassy Moves in Public

1. Applying lipstick or lipliner.
2. Chewing on toothpicks.
3. Clipping or filing fingernails.
4. Chewing on nails.
5. Brushing your hair
6. Picking your nose
7. Telling sexual or diversity related jokes
8. Burping.
9. Talking with food in your mouth
10. (Men) repositioning yourself

Physical Imperfections

Attraction can be physical and usually accompanies first impressions. What attracts you to someone is their presentation of what they have or rather their interpretation of life as seen through their expression.

You like the way a woman wears her hair rather than the hair itself, and you like the way she holds her hands, or uses them to gesture rather than just the hands themselves.

Most people have imperfect bodies which is just fine, that makes you all the more human, but that shouldn't stump your self-esteem.

In this era of eternal youth and cosmetic surgery it is easy to get confused and think that beauty is only skin deep, or that there is merit in adding or subtracting to your body parts. This is erroneous thinking because if you are not happy with yourself before you spend big bucks on alterations, you will not be happy with yourself after.

Certainly make the most of what you have physically, take care to exercise and eat healthy and be sensible about the weight you carry, but part of psychological health is realizing that physical change takes time.

If you want to drop a few pounds that is okay too, but love yourself today in the process. Find enjoyment and pleasure in your activities and don't wait until you lose the weight to feel good about yourself.

> *"He who has health has hope,*
> *He who has hope has everything."*
> *- Arabian proverb*

When you accept yourself as you are, you give others permission to accept you as well.

How to Achieve Physical Balance

Did you ever see someone who looked healthy? I mean they just radiate vibrant energy.

Working out will do that to you. Aerobics, running, brisk walking, swimming, skiing, cycling, and skating are all cardiovascular exercises that circulate your blood and stimulate your mind. Spend time each day working out.

Other benefits of exercising:
- Calm nerves
- Self-confidence
- Natural high (endorphin release)
- Blood sugar equalization
- Muscle strength
- Appetite control
- Sleep patterns regulated
- Burn calories

It may not be fun to workout in the beginning but it is a great way to release stress and pressure from work or home. Exercise can be done in front of the TV with an inexpensive video instructor or you can purchase a variety of exercise packages from a local gym. While it is not essential that you work out at a gym, it has been proven that more people actually work out when they drop what they are doing and get away from the TV, the refrigerator and all the other stuff that consumes time and energy at home.

Either way, block out daily exercise time a month in advance on your calendar when getting started, so you make sure you have the time to create a new you.

Exercising at a gym will connect you with others who share similar athletic and health interests. It is also a great place to network and sponsor people. This gives you a chance to follow up with them during your workouts instead of spending business time to accomplish the same thing.

Make it a point to hang out and exercise with people who can show you proper movements. This prevents injury and unnecessary pulled muscles. Find people who inspire you to workout each day, and hold you accountable for your progress.

There are days when you will not feel like working out and just showing up at the gym resets your attitude to one hundred percent. It is kind of like rebooting a computer that has crashed. You go from blah to a great attitude in no time flat.

Success Reminders

- Who you are, the ways you dress, the way you carry yourself, are all advertisements for your business.

- Being pressed is the difference between looking like a hundredaire and a millionaire.

- Distractions in clothes take away from personal power.

- Wear only clothes that represent you and the message you are trying to send.

- Accessories are intended to enhance your natural beauty, not cover it.

- When you accept yourself as you are, you give others permission to accept you as well.

Chapter 4:

Self-Confidence

Everyone covets confidence. It is an attitude, a conviction, a "mind-set" that is so powerful it can make you believe you can fly. And it is essential to your success as a distributor. At the other extreme, it can disappear so completely that it can make you too terrified to get out of bed in the morning – which can be the demise of your business.

Confidence is developed, as you become sure of yourself. You reach a place where you finally know without a doubt how you will respond in the face of adversity, or what you will say when you are faced with confrontation. It is knowing you can count on yourself under all situations and under all circumstances, and you know others can count on you too.

> *"Act as if what you do makes a difference, it does."*
> *– William James*

With self-confidence, you feel successful and free to take on projects that will skyrocket your small business. And as you build on your existing confidence, you will find others have confidence in you as well. This confidence will keep building on itself until you are truly unstoppable.

How to Boost Self-Confidence

Begin by realizing there is only one you.

You are not in competition with anyone else. Life is not a race or a round you can win, similarly, you cannot lose. Just wake-up every day, and know that you get to spend your whole day with you. Are you the kind of person you would want to spend today with?

If not, make a note of one or two things you can do today to become the kind of person you would want to spend today with.

Do you have a personal game plan to improve?

Are your values in harmony with your beliefs?

Are you connected spiritually?

Do you spend quality time with your family?

Are you eating healthy foods?

Are you getting enough sleep at night?

Are you exercising on a day-to-day basis?

Are you reading books that improve your mind?

Are you networking on regular basis?

Are you returning telephone calls and emails?

Are you taking prospects with you to your weekly business opportunity meetings?

Self-confidence will improve when you improve.

All of these things and more add to your self-confidence. When you like yourself, others like you too, and when others like you, you like yourself more. It is a perpetual cycle that allows you to learn, grow, and enjoy the process.

Learn to present your ideas to other people in a manner that is consistent with your beliefs. You are more likely to be heard and believed if your message is congruent with your actions.

If you need help learning to present your ideas, join Toastmasters.

Toastmasters is an international organization, with clubs all across the country. Most clubs meet once a week for the benefit of self-improvement.

Club meetings are divided into three sections: prepared speeches, extemporaneous speeches, and evaluations.

When you join toastmasters, there is a form to fill out a fee to pay. The form is simple and the fee is a great investment. Eighteen US dollars every six months plus some clubs have a small dues fee that includes the cost of the weekly meeting room.

$18.00 divided by 6 months is $3.00 a month for continuing education. That is about .75 cents a week (less than a cup of coffee) for hands on practice that will turn your public speaking fears of yesterday into business profit and self-confidence today.

The Power of Prepared Speaking

When you join Toastmasters, you are given a manual that walks you through your first ten prepared speeches. The manual helps you focus on elements of a great speech such as vocal variety, eye contact, speaking in a cohesive manner, speaking with sincerity, being persuasive and so on.

Learning to speak in public and present ideas is a great idea in any profession, but especially in small business and network marketing where you will be making a living by presenting your ideas to others.

Chatting Your Way to a Sale

The second part of the Toastmaster meeting with extemporaneous speaking is fun, and teaches you to think on your feet. This section of the meeting is generally called "Table Topics" and there is a Table Topics master who picks somebody out of the audience randomly and then proceeds to ask them a question. If she picks you, you get to answer the question (totally off the cuff) to the audience for two or three minutes. This teaches you to think in a logical manner without preparation on something you or may not know a thing about.

As you improve in table topics, you will find yourself with increased confidence and the ability to answer objections of every sort from prospects that may have preconceived ideas about the company that you are promoting.

Evaluations vs. Objections

The evaluations portion of the meeting is extremely helpful as a Toastmaster evaluates your prepared speech.

"Hey Harry, I liked the manner in which you presented your ideas, but I felt as if you spoke too fast which made me dizzy while I tried to comprehend what you were saying."

This is VERY helpful information as you use the suggestions from the last meeting for your next speech.

You will also find yourself improving on the suggestions in your sales presentations, your weekly business opportunity meeting presentations, your product demonstrations and so on.
The evaluation portion of the meeting is intended to help you reconstruct your ideas so that you become a master at the art of presenting.

As you learn to present your ideas in public (and Toastmasters is a weekly place for you to practice) your self-confidence will skyrocket.

Get a copy of the local Business Journal and go to the "Calendar" section and there will be a listing of all the Toastmasters clubs in your area along with the times of day they meet, location and contact information of the person in charge.
Most Toastmasters clubs allow you to visit free three or four meetings free of charge and without commitment, to see if you like the forum and the people involved. I strongly recommend it.

In addition, you can go to www.toastmasters.org for more information on a Toastmasters club near you.

How to Create a Belief System

> *"Risk more than others think is safe.*
> *Care more than others think is wise.*
> *Dream more than others think is practical.*
> *Expect more than others think is possible."*
> *- Cadet Maxim*

There will be days in the business, as there are in any business, when the fun is gone. Bills are due and no one is buying what you are selling. You are having sensitivities and your business team is challenging you at every turn. Suddenly your dream becomes a blurry nightmare and you want to throw in the towel and quit the business. You might even find yourself asking: "Why am I putting myself through this?"

Here is your answer: *Because you are worth it.*

When you experience moments of self-doubt, remind yourself of these things:

- You already have what it takes to launch an uncommon dream.

- Your dream does not require the approval of those you love.

- No one can stop a man with a plan because no one has a plan to stop him.

- You are worth the upgrade in lifestyle that a new opportunity can provide.

- Those who believe in your dreams will be instantly energized and encouraged.

- Anything neglected will deteriorate. Don't let it be the dream of your life.

- Remember life will eventually catch you on the downside. This is the time you need to concentrate your energy.

Tips to Keep Yourself Motivated

1. Associate with those whose fire is presently burning brighter than your own.

2. Ask for help when you need it.

3. Find someone to re-inspire you when necessary.

4. Review with your business support team the reasons why you are a distributor. If your support team is a good distance away from you, call them or email them. If you have lost touch with your organization or group, you can actually do the review yourself.

5. Get some paper and a pen, or do this on your computer. Make two lists. On the first list, note all the reasons why you went into business for yourself and all of the benefits you are receiving as an independent business owner. On the other side of the paper make a list of the challenges or "to do's" to get back on track. Reminding yourself of your reason why you chose to be a distributor will keep you inspired and motivated.

6. Next, make a list of all your personal assets. Take an inventory of who you are and what you bring to your business.
   Your list might look something like this:
   - *I am enthusiastic.*
   - *I am energetic.*
   - *I have youth on my side.*
   - *I am reasonable.*
   - *I can think logically through difficult decisions.*
   - *I am friendly and attract positive people into my life.*
   - *I enjoy working with my friends and they enjoy working with me.*
   - *I am a self-starter…and so on.*

Once you determine your skills, it is easy to determine where to focus your business energy.

7. In your review, look at your work habits. Be real with yourself. Are you really working all the time you are working-or are you piddling away a large part of every day getting ready to do the business?

> *"Men are anxious to improve their circumstances,*
> *Yet unwilling to improve themselves;*
> *Therefore they remain bound. "*
> *– James Allen*

- Have completeness in your work.
- Work the whole time you work.
- Play the whole time you are playing
- Relax the whole time you are relaxing.

One of the biggest struggles of small business ownership is the faulty thinking that you are always working. No one is always working. You might be busy most of the time, but are you productive? You might consider taking time out to rest and relax and when you begin working again, you will be alert and have a greater clarity of mind.

- Allow yourself time off just as if this were a regular job and you were punching a time clock.
- Make time for yourself and block it out each day.

- Take time to eat. Eat at your dinner table without the TV, newspaper, computer or telephone. Focus on eating when you are eating.

- Sleep when you are sleeping. Turn off the TV, radio, lights etc. Sleep is for rest and relaxation and while you are sleeping, your mind will digest all you have learned during the day, sort it out and find solutions. This is hard to accomplish when there is music, and other distractions for your mind to sort through.

How to Get Out of a Slump

If you reach an obstacle in your business and are not certain of what to do next, use the HALT method.

Never make a major decision when you are:

Hungry

Angry

Lonely

Tired

None of these decisions made in this frame of mind are likely to be wise.

If you remain in a slump for more than a few minutes, pull out your positive attitude tapes. If you don't have any, invest in some. You can find them regional rallies and often your business support team has access to such tapes.

You will eventually want to create your own success library and fill it with motivational tapes and books used for slumps and regular daily reminders.

Listen to these tapes on your way to meetings, presentations and before you show the plan. They will keep your spirits bright and give you great ideas to cut your learning curve.

> *"A businessman's judgement is no better than his information."*
> *– P.R. Lamont*

Other people in your organization might have purchased tapes and you can do a tape swap so you are continually learning the latest information revolving around your business and success.

Libraries are also a great resource - most offer a free library card and allow you to check up to 50 books out at a time.

Check the Internet, it is possible now at some libraries to check the library databases online and order books through the Internet using your library card as a pass code. Then the local librarian pulls the books you requested and you simply drive through much like you would a fast food restaurant and pick up your books at the window.
The loan of most books through your public library is free and they let you borrow books for two to three weeks.
Make it a personal goal to read every book in your public library on marketing, sales and motivation.

Another great resource to pull you out of a slump is other successful people in your industry who have been where you are. They know the ropes and know what you might be going through.
Ask them what their staying motivated secrets are, you might be surprised what you hear. Some meditate some exercise, some review their goals, some take a vacation and others just keep repeating the basics.

If you are in a slump because money is tight and you're only a paycheck or two ahead of catastrophe, remember it consumes more energy to juggle your way around payments, than it does to get out and earn new money. Don't get stuck on the financial tightrope of asking your creditors for extensions while you are praying for a miracle. Just get out there and do the work. And no matter how tough things get, continually hold in your mind the picture of personal prosperity.

> *"Worry does not empty tomorrow of its sorrow;*
> *It empties today of its strength. "*
> *– Charles Spurgeon*

Another reason independent business owners sink into slumps or get discouraged is because they listen to negative talkers. Realize that some people in life get their sense of accomplishment and achievement from trying to stop others.

Don't put too much stock in those people who would bring you down out of jealousy or envy. Instead, focus on creating a life that is nurtured by those who believe in you.

Chances are if you are in the business long enough, you will find someone who will want to crush your enthusiasm for success and personal development. It might be a well intending family member, friend, relative who only "cares for your best interests" and can't stand the thought of you frittering away your life to something they don't understand.

And while it is easy to see that they care for you, it is not as easy to withstand their negativity.

Learn to accept and love people for who they are without letting them destroy you and your dream.

Success Reminders

- With self-confidence, you feel successful and free to take on projects that will skyrocket your small business.

- Realize there is only one you. You are not in competition with anyone else.

- Self-confidence will improve when you improve.

- Learning to speak in public and present ideas is a great idea in any profession, but especially in small business and network marketing where you will be making a living by presenting your ideas to others.

- Your dream does not require the approval of those you love.

- You are worth the upgrade in lifestyle that a new opportunity can provide.

- Anything neglected will deteriorate. Don't let it be the dream of your life.

- Associate with those whose fire is presently burning brighter than your own.

- Ask for help when you need it.

- Men are anxious to improve their circumstances, yet unwilling to improve themselves, therefore they remain bound.

- Learn to become the person that you like to be around and others will want to be around you too.

- No one can stop a man with a plan because no one has a plan to stop him.

- There are only about eight or ten objections that ever come up in any sale. Learn eight or ten good answers that address those objections.

- HALT when you need to make a major decision and never make one when you are Hungry, Angry, Lonely or Tired.

- Remember it consumes more energy trying to juggle payments around to prevent paying something than it does to actually earn new money.

Chapter 5:

Networking Made Easy

The Best Place to Find Prospects

The best place to find prospects, this may sound strange, is where you are. Regardless of where you are, if others are around, participating in similar activities, it stands to reason you have something in common with them.

For example, let's suppose you go to a hotel and ride the elevator up to the fifteenth floor. Instead of riding up in silence – a common question you might ask another person in the elevator is:

"Are you here on business or pleasure?"

Because most people don't go to hotels in their hometown and ride up and down the elevators. Therefore, it is fairly safe to assume he is from out of town. The next question may be: "where are you from?" "How is the weather there?" or you can discuss the sports team in his hometown.

Suppose you meet a woman on the way out of a seminar. A common question might be: "Do you attend lectures like this often?" Regardless of the answer, you could follow it with, "Who is the best speaker you have heard recently?" Soon you find yourself in conversation.

Everyone sharing the same time and space with you automatically has something in common with you. Learn to take advantage of common moments.

Network Outside Your Comfort Zone

Chamber of Commerce meetings, Toastmaster meetings, Kiwanis club meetings, Lions club meetings, PTA meetings, Neighborhood Watch meetings are all good places to meet prospects for your business.

However, you want to remain tactful when attending meetings for the sole purpose of finding people to sponsor. You do not want to appear as if you are there just to recruit bodies.

Recruiting during inopportune times can create ill will within an association and attributes to the black eye many MLM and networking companies have. Learn to be a distributor who improves the image of the company you are promoting—not a distributor who detracts.

So how do you network without being perceived as an angler looking for the next bite? The answer is simple, you have to get involved and look and act as if you are part of the equation for the success of the meeting.

- Go to the meetings early.

- Volunteer to help set up chairs and tables.

- Volunteer to help with registration.

- Volunteer to help with punch and cookies if served.

- Volunteer to help the speaker set up flip charts, television or internet connections or get them a drink of water in case they get thirsty while speaking.
- Greet people as they enter and thank them for attending the meeting. Ask them the reason they came and what they are hoping to learn as a result of attending?

- Network gracefully (asking questions and listening for answers that qualify your prospects throughout the meeting.)

- Be the last one to leave the meeting.

- Volunteer to put away chairs.

- Volunteer to pick up extra handouts or clean up excess stuff left as a result of the meeting.

- Volunteer to take the speaker to the airport or make sure they have a ride to their hotel.

- Once you have made some wonderful contacts, make sure you follow up with your new friends immediately following the meeting.

One distributor carried with her to community meetings a small wicker basket filled with 15 business cards. She appointed herself the "official door prize committee chairperson". The 15 business cards were to create the illusion that your card was not the first card in her basket. She never asked you for a card, but as you entered the room, she greeted you and shook your hand while holding the basket in her other hand. Almost automatically, people would reach in their pockets and add a business card to her collection.

Although this was not a business opportunity meeting, and often she was not part of the program, they would still introduce her and have come to the front of the room.

As they introduced her, (it was a free commercial to let everyone know what she did for a living.) she was able to share her sales pitch with the entire room at once.)
And as she came forward, she smiled and made eye contact with those whom she had greeted at the door. It was as if everyone in the room were her friend.
With her she brought her wicker basket and proceeded to draw a name from it. Graciously she would award the winner a door prize such as a coffee mug filled with chocolate - that she herself provided. The host of the meeting appreciated her thoughtfulness and she appreciated the opportunity to be recognized in front of the entire room, as well as take home a basket of business cards for later reference.

That afternoon, (or the following morning) she entered all of the business cards into her computerized Rolodex. She then mail merged on the back of a personal photo post card a nice note about how she enjoyed meeting you at the community meeting that day. Still she was not selling anything, Nor did she have the time to personally follow up with a hundred plus people for every meeting she attended, but she created an enormous network based on perception alone.
She was immediately recognized on the photo post card because personally had greeted all of the guests as they entered the meeting, and then they saw her up at the front of the room as she awarded a door prize to a very lucky winner.

From there, she occasionally followed up with newsletters or post-cards from her travels and then as the internet became popular she added to her prospecting a free weekly e-newsletter.

She was never pushy or demanding in her connections, rather she created a friendly environment where people wanted to participate in whatever she was doing, whether it was business related or involvement with the community.

Network Naturally

There are as many ways to network as there are various personalities. Don't worry if what I am recommending doesn't fit your personality or style, find a way that works for you.

Observe people who have a personality similar to yours and make them your mentor. Find out what is working for them and if it works for you, go ahead and duplicate it. If your networking seems stressed and uncomfortable to you and your prospects, change what you are doing until it becomes second nature to you and you feel comfortable enough to make your prospects comfortable.

Remember Names

People like to be remembered. It is said that "the most beautiful sound a person will every hear is their own name." Make it a point as part of your professional development to remember names and faces. When you see a familiar face (even if you can't remember their name), you can say, "Hey it's good to see you again." Still try to make the person to whom you are talking feel important and recognized. Then politely ask their name and repeat it in your mind three times to capture it in your memory.

Pocket Promotions

If you do not have a business card, get one. They are easy to create now even on a home computer and can help drive traffic to your website. Carry them with you wherever you go. You never know when you will meet someone who will want to get back in touch with you.

Have a coupon, discount for a product, or some other offer on the back of your business card so people have an incentive to call you.

Go Early—Stay Late

When attending a networking function get there early. Be there when the doors open and volunteer to help if possible. The people who are running the event will appreciate your help and the regular guests who are arriving will assume you are on the committee. Stay late until the last person leaves. Just network, network, network. Some of the best contacts you will ever make will be on their way out to the parking lot last.

Follow-up

Follow up with people you just met in the non-threatening and friendly way. You can never have too many friends. Think of your prospects as friends and not chances for you to make money. Sincere interest in people will be appreciated and will create more money in your organization than any slick sales tactics ever will. If you appear to be out "scouting for dollars" your prospects will sense that as well and you both lose.

Listen

Whenever you meet someone, listen to them talk before you tell them all about you. When you show a genuine awareness in others, they feel that you are interested and interesting.

After you have gathered pertinent information ask power questions that involve the other person and give you valuable information and insight about which, that will qualify them for your business.

> *"Of all the things you wear,*
> *Your expression is the most important."*
> *- Jane Lane*

Smile if you're a Winner

Have you ever walked through an amusement park, a shopping mall, or grocery store, and noticed that many people instead of smiling and enjoying the day, appear as if they are slugging through a mud pit.

People forget to smile. They look worried, sick, bored and tired with life.

You are different. You love life and all it has to offer, so show it.

Take a deep breath and stand up straight. Smile with all your teeth and enjoy the magic each moment provides. Rest your top teeth on your bottom lip. I promise it is contagious. You know those miserable people who hate to smile when they are bored and angry? Well you are going to wreck havoc to their day.

They are going to look at you and wonder where you have been and if there's any left. Smile at people and watch how many of them smile back. It is a friendly way of exchanging a silent message that says, "I am a winner."

The Art of Personal Magnetism

Personal magnetism is derived from enthusiasm. Show enthusiasm for life, for health, wealth and prosperity. Exhibit an enthusiasm for the choices to be active, alive and thriving. Enthusiasm is not obnoxious or loud. It is alarmingly poised, yet others will catch it through the shine in your eyes and the rhythm of your step. Enthusiasm is a gift you give freely, and those who receive it do so enthusiastically. The magnet that attracts others to you is a reflection of hope. People see you at your best and they unconsciously say to themselves: "He's got something I want".

People like you though they often do not know why. They just know that they want to hang out in your space. They want to eat what you are eating, wear what you are wearing and say the words you say.

The secret is not at all, about what you do…it is about whom you are, it is what you believe, and how you use what you believe to positively impact the lives of others.

How to Develop Personal Magnetism

Look around you. Who is the coolest person you know? And what is it about them that is so charming? Is it the way they carry themselves? Or perhaps you are attracted to the fact that a friend only says positive things about others. You might like the way a person admits when they are wrong and not afraid to apologize if they have hurt your feelings. You might like the sincerity of a person when they are passionate about a particular belief. Whatever the behavior is try this:

- For one week, carry a small note pad and a pen and take notes about the people around you. Make a list of their attributes that stand out.

- At the end of the week, take the list of wonderful manners you have uncovered and begin implementing them in your personal life.

- Do not copy any one particular person or try to become them – simply use them as an example.

- Be authentically you, just tweak your own behaviors and attitudes until they become attractive to others. If you emulate the kind of person you want to hang out with, you will soon draw similar people into your life and your organization.

Good Gossip

Some call it promotion others call it gossip. Regardless of the name, you call it; the bottom line is people will talk about you. And you have chosen a business and a lifestyle that supports people talking about you, in front of you and behind your back.

> *"Time will expose or promote you." – Jim Rohn*

Whether they say nice or negative stuff will determine whether they expose or promote you. Live your life so when people talk about you they are promoting you and your cause. This is the time to watch your language, behavior, promises, work ethic and values.

Because yours is a business of duplication, your business team will duplicate in their own organizations the same behaviors they see in you.

- Learn not to make promises you cannot keep. People judge you on your actions, not your intentions. Under all circumstances do what you say you are going to do, only then are you counted on at all times.

- Learn to hold your tongue when frustrated, angry or upset. It is difficult to retain clarity of thought, charisma and professionalism when you're stomping about, rolling your eyes and cursing. Anger is a common emotion that should be addressed, though in the proper time and place, and only after you're well rested.

- Learn to keep secrets. Work every day for the rest of your life to become known as a person who can be trusted to keep a tale to yourself. You do not endear anyone by gossip, slander or sharing a story that does not belong to you. If someone trusts you enough to be vulnerable with you, and share with you something in confidence, respect that. Be savvy enough to spread hope, not stories of despair and gloom.

Understand that eventually in life, somewhere along the way, someone will say something that defames you. It might be something slanderous or disbelieving of your intentions. Learn not to take it personally, such things are often said out of envy and jealousy. Understand that part of human nature is the need to elevate oneself above others. Some people will bring you down in a heartbeat if they have the chance just to make themselves look a little taller under the present light.

Life is way too short, and you are way too important to chase down, and argue with somebody who has spoken ill of you. So, if you hear a negative rumor someone is spreading about you, let go of it and do not let it consume your precious energy and enthusiasm. Just focus every day on giving life your best and the best will come back to you.

Edify Others

Sarcasm and gossip are cheap and can be obtained at the check out counter of most grocery stores. However, the person who builds others instead of tearing them down is respected far more than he who tells a juicy tale.

Go out of your way to find something nice to say about the people you work with, the people you live with and those who surround you from day to day. Subconsciously, those in your realm of influence will determine that you look for the best in others and they will feel that you will find the best in them too. We all want to hang out with people who encourage us not crush our spirits with criticism.

Recognition

People need to be needed and recognized. When you solicit the help of others, you will find most of the time; they are more then willing to help you. And when others do help you, find ways to recognize them in public. This empowers them to continue helping you. Psychology 101 teaches us that the behaviors we reward will be repeated (either positive or negative.) So when we go out of our way to make mention of the things we see being done correctly, we inspire that continuing behavior.

Long Term Networking

Remember the people you meet today, will most likely still be around in ten or fifteen years from now. As life's circumstances change, people change jobs and positions but they do not usually just go away.

Be nice to everyone because you never know when the temp or the administrative assistant working in a local firm will turn out to be the major CEO in a corporation ten years down the road. They may even end up your best superstar.
Don't prejudge people, and if someone is not interested in your opportunity today, their situation may one-day change, and they will want to work with you. Treat all people with the respect they truly deserve regardless of their position in life, one day they may return to help you.

Success Reminders

- The best place to find prospects is where you are. Regardless of your location, if others are participating in similar activities, it stands to reason you have something in common with them.

- Go to meetings and networking events early.

- Volunteer to help set up chairs and tables and put them away after the event has concluded.

- Volunteer to help with registration or greet people at the door.

- Volunteer to help with refreshments if served.

- Volunteer to help the speaker set up flip charts, television or internet connections or get them water in case they get thirsty while speaking.

- Network gracefully (asking questions and listening for answers that qualify your prospects throughout the meeting.)

- Be the last one to leave the meeting.

- Volunteer to pick up extra handouts or clean up excess stuff left as a result of the meeting.

- Volunteer to take the speaker to the airport or make sure they have a ride to their hotel.

- Once you have made some wonderful contacts, be certain to follow up with your new friends immediately following the meeting.

- Be authentically you in all your dealings.

- Think of your friends as friends and not chances for you to make money—this will bring you *more* friends *and* more money.

- Remember Names and Faces. People like to be remembered.

- Be the kind of person you want to sponsor and automatically you will attract similar people to you.

- Time will expose or promote you, live so others are promoting you and your cause.

Chapter 6:

Best Follow Up Methods

Suppose you want to follow up with a good prospect, or people in your group, yet your business is not moving at lightening speed and to call your friends and prospects regularly might make you seem desperate for business or turn you into a pest.

Here are a few for starters:

Top Ten List

Send a top ten list highlighting your prospects interests or hobbies. There are scads of top ten lists that have been written and many web pages built around them. Some are comical, while others are helpful hints and tips that will save your prospects time and money. With a little research, you are sure to find some that are applicable to your prospects personal interests.

Have a Contest

Have a contest and give away a prize or an award. It does not have to be expensive, but it does have to be well advertised within your organization. You can have a contest for just about any reason. It can be based around productivity within your group, web site hits, referrals, how many guests your distributors bring to weekly business opportunity meetings, how many people they sponsor into your group within a certain period of time and so on.

Advertise the rules on your web site, in your e-newsletters, on telephone messages, and at your business opportunity meetings. Contests are fun, they create friendly competition and inspire inactive distributors off dead center while motivating prospects to join you in business.

Carry a Camera

After you have a lucky winner for your contest, make certain you take plenty of pictures. Get a photo of you awarding the winner his prize. Send the photo and a small blurb about the award to the local Business Journal for publication. They love to recognize small businesses on the move. Publish the picture on your web site and use it for future promotions and future contests you will be holding in the near future.

The Power of Postcards

One distributor created postcards from photos. Wherever she went she met people and collected their business cards. Then she would follow up with a picture post card and people recognized her again when they saw her.

Many contact software programs now allow you to mail merge contact information and addresses onto a simple post card. Let's say you meet 30 people on Monday at a community meeting, that evening, you could compose a personalized greeting card and mail merge all the names and addresses.

Everyone gets a card from you and they think because their name and address was printed on it, that you personally took the time to write all of the people.

Mail merging is easy now with some email database programs and it is easier than ever to attach a photo of yourself so the prospect will remember you when they open the email. Or you can direct them to your web site that also has photos of you.

Drop By

You have heard the old "thought I'd drop by, I was in the neighborhood". Well, it still works today in networking. It is polite if you have a cell telephone, to call on your way over so they can put on a pot of tea.

Electronically Drop By

Today in cyberspace, it is easy to instant message your prospects and business support team. Many of the Internet service providers have the capabilities to show you when your friends are live on the internet.

If you see your friends are surfing the web, you can drop them an instant message and send a short "Greetings".

Send a Coupon

One distributor who loves ice cream gives away transferable coupons to his local ice cream store – the only caveat was you had to eat your ice cream with him. If your schedule would not permit you to join him for ice cream, perhaps you would be so kind to pass along your coupon. This gave him someone to share 30 minutes with at the ice cream store that possibly had not heard yet about his opportunity.

Magazine Run

Another distributor who subscribed to tons of magazines would read her incoming magazines, then do a weekly magazine run and drop off each magazine (to a friend she knew had similar interests) while she was out running errands. She might drop off a health magazine to her triathlete friend, a clothing magazine to her fashion-conscious friend, a cooking magazine to a house mom and so on. It was a lovely excuse to "catch up" with out the threat of her trying to recruit them.

Referral Discounts

One business man referred his friends to people he'd had positive experiences doing business with in his local community. He would tell his prospects and friends: "Go see John over at XYZ company and ask him for the Bob Powers (insert your own name) Discount. Tell him you're a friend of mine and he'll really take care of you." This shows John (a prospect) that Bob Powers (who is trying to sponsor him) is out recommending other business his way. Next time you drop in to see John, he will surely take time to visit with you. When you show a local business owner that you respect their entre-preneurialism and business judgments by referring business their way, they in turn will show you respect for yours by doing the same.

Weekly Drawing

Give something away. One distributor called a prospect that was too busy to see him to tell him he was the winner of lunch at a certain restaurant. He then told the prospect he had to claim the lunch that week which day was best? He would swing by and pick up his prospect and together they would go to lunch. At the end of the lunch, the guy picked up the meal tab- making it free to the prospect. This gave him a chance to share his opportunity with the prospect during lunch - at no cost to the prospect.

If you choose to do a similar drawing, make sure it is well advertised. When you drop off product orders to your regular customers, have a list of lunch winners taped to your delivery. This keeps them informed of what is happening in your business and allows them to share in your excitement and growth.

Write Press Releases

A press release is a short informational article usually written in third party that explains you or your business opportunity. When writing one, focus on the benefits of working with you or your group, yet maintain a fair sense of objectivity.

Send your release to local papers or newsletters for publication. After they have been published print copies and include them in all your mailings, newsletters and on your website.

This is a great way to inform friends and prospects about updates in your business.

Success Reminders

- Having a contest involves prospects and distributors and creates a continual excitement that breeds momentum & growth.

- Drop by electronically or by post card to your prospects and business support team. It is hard to do business with someone you've forgotten.

- Give your used magazines away to people with similar interests as a chance to visit those who normally wouldn't speak with you about your opportunity. It gives you another chance to be fact to face.

- Show a local business owner that you respect their entrepreneurialism and business judgments by referring business their way, they in turn will show you respect for yours by doing the same.

- Send a press release to local papers or newsletters for publication. Print copies and include them in all your mailings, newsletters and on your website. This is a great way to inform friends and prospects about updates in your business.

- Create an award and then promote the winner in your local paper. You both benefit from the publicity.

- Carry a camera. When you get the film developed, send your prospect a picture of the two of you with a note and an update about your business.

- Turn your photo into a picture post card for follow up notes and networking.

Chapter 7:

The Power of Meetings

Why Go to Meetings?

People go to meetings for a variety of reasons such as: obligation, curiosity, greed, affiliation, likability, problem solving. The electricity of a crowd is infectious. Many of your associates will be motivated by these events, and they will make stronger commitments to achieve their goals. If you are having a bum week, you need to go to meetings to be re-energized and if you are on top of the world, someone in your group needs to see you at the meeting.

Remember this is a business led by example. Your business team will duplicate what they see you doing. If they see you attending meetings regularly, they will attend meetings as well. If they know you are in town and you have put a picnic above the priority of a business opportunity meeting, they will know it is not important for them to attend the meetings either. If no one in your group is going to meetings, your business dissolves.

The Power of Mirror Marketing

Have you ever noticed other people during business opportunity meetings? If the speaker says something important and you take notes – often the people sitting near you are watching you out of the corner of their eye and they see you taking notes, so they take notes as well.

This secret almost always works.

Suppose you have a new prospect with you at a meeting, and the speaker is talking. If you want to reemphasize a particular point, nod your head in agreement.

Even if you know the speech backwards and forwards, if the speaker makes an important point, make sure you are taking notes. Your new prospect will think "hey he's been to lots of these meetings and so he knows what is important, and I see him taking notes, so I guess this is something I should remember". And like magic, they will take notes as well.

If you are watching a company video with a prospect and they interrupt to ask a question, the same rules apply. They are watching your body language and how you respond to the information being presented. Hold up one finger as if you are saying "hold on a second". And continue watching the video. This sends the signal that the information you are viewing is of utmost importance and then they will pay attention by mirroring your behavior.

You are also training them what to do with their prospects.

If you are in somebody's house watching a video or doing a computer presentation on email, pay full attention to what you are doing. When you stop to pet their cat or read posters on their walls, you send a signal that other things are more important than your time there. Focus, teach your prospects to focus and they will teach their prospects and new recruits to do the same.

Divide Your Influence

Suppose you go to a weekly business opportunity meeting with your spouse and you have eleven prospects visiting and thirteen existing distributors in the room. Instead of sitting with your spouse during the meeting, divide your energy. Spread yourselves throughout the group. Let your spouse work half the room and you work the other half answering questions, asking questions and making yourself available to your group.

The same rule applies if you are in a community meeting not designated for networking purposes. Split up and network half of the room while your business partner, spouse, children, distributors work the other half. When you get back together, you can share your leads, exchange ideas and so on.

Make it a rule to never sit by people you know during meetings. Get to know the other people who are there.

What Have You Got To Loose?

Sometimes we become intimidated when we meet a seemingly "big-hitter". We feel that his friends are more important than we are and we should not interfere with his or her time so we forget to treat them like business associates. We forget to invite them to meetings with us for fear that they might say no and then we will have "lost" them as a distributor.

The reality is, you are not going to lose them, because in reality, you do not have them signed on as a distributor yet anyway. How can you lose something you do not have?

Also, when you are afraid you will lose the sale if you ask the prospect to buy - you have already lost it--or rather you never had it.

In other words, you have nothing to lose and everything to gain by asking your prospects and customers to buy your products and attend your meetings.

Change your attitude today and realize big hitters became big hitters because they have learned to make informed business decisions. If they say yes, good for you, and f they say no, good for you too because now you are not frittering away your precious time wondering if they will or they will not choose your opportunity. At lease if they say no, you are free to move on and approach the next heavy hitter.

Volunteer

Visibility is the key. In a community meeting, or any meeting for that matter, learn to be seen. Ask if you can introduce the speaker. Offer to give announcements at the end of the meeting. Volunteer to give away a door prize. Volunteer to pass out handouts. Greet people as they enter the room. Thank people and invite them back as they leave the meeting. The thing to remember is you are going to be at the meeting anyway. Your helping out is not going to take any more time than you would already be spending.

Use meeting time to help out and be seen.

Create a Competitive Edge

One genius marketer and high-class recruiter, made it a point to be seen at every meeting she attended. If it cost fifteen bucks for registration at a meeting, she would pay just like any one else. The difference with Angela was she would get their 15 minutes early and stand right inside the entry door. She appointed herself the "official greeter" of the meeting.

"Hi, I am Angela, and I am so glad you could make it today" she would say in a warm and friendly tone a she reached to shake hands.

"Come right over here to the registration table and we'll get you a name badge."

The new person being shy and quiet would be led naturally into conversation as she asked them, "tell me, are you from around here?" If another distributor brought a guest she would first greet the known distributor and allow them to introduce their guest.

Both were made to feel welcome as she directed them to the registration table.

Without ever saying it, everyone assumed she was on a committee of some sort. When it came time to leave the meeting people would go find Angela assuming she was the person they needed to thank for a good time. In addition, she, in her warm and friendly style would say "I am so glad you could make it to tonight's meeting, you know you're really lucky to be working with Bill. He's one of our biggest superstars." She would edify whoever brought the guest and was gracious to all.

Other than being instantly liked by everybody, she was perceived as a leader in the organization.

People flocked around her wanting to be a part of whatever she was doing. This was profitable at community events where everybody was a prospect for her networking business.

> *How sad to wander through life thinking*
> *"Life's a party and I'm the guest."*
> *When you could take responsibility instead as the host.*
> *– Angela Brown*

Wu Wei

The Chinese have developed a philosophy that transcends our western culture and teaches us to "allow all things to be". It is futile to be angry at something or someone for fulfilling their nature.

Allowing all things to be is to realize that a tree is a tree. A tree provides shade. And while a tree has the potential of being chopped down and it is limbs being rearranged into the form of a chair, the tree is a tree, and NOT a chair.
We must not allow ourselves to get confused into thinking that the tree will eventually become a chair simply because it has the potential.

Similarly, a chair is a chair. It provides a place to sit not the shade of a tree. It is a waste of energy to be upset with the chair for not providing shade and angry the tree does not give us a place to sit.

The same philosophy applies to folks you may sponsor into your group. You may have sponsored at one time somebody with a burning passion for being a distributor. Since then (for whatever reason), their fire has dwindled to mere smoke. They are busy doing stuff so they look as if they are smoking; however, there is no fire.

And while there is *potential* for a fire, you don't have the energy or the resources to keep igniting them. You can stop doing your business trying to convince them to do theirs. You can bribe, beg, and re-explain your dreams to them, but in the end, they are trees and not chairs, smoke but not fire.

Learn to recognize that some distributors with the brightest potential will never make it in this business. Some are just right down too smart. They have too much importance to be successful. They already have all the answers (which have nothing to do with what works) and you cannot tell them anything or teach them anything. Allow them to be - and move on.

There are also people who will follow you around and copy what you do. They have not a clue what works and they will believe anything you tell them, and then they do not know any better than to go implement it. And presto! You have a superstar in the making.

Create an environment within your group that supports the best in everybody. Celebrate the shade of the trees and the seats of the chairs but do not try to make a person into something that is unnatural to their nature.

I will encourage you to give life your best because life deserves your best, and you deserve the best from life. Live up to your fullest potential because there is no glory in living small.
At the same time, I am also advising you to stop chasing prospects and distributors who are not ready for success.
You cannot force success - it can only happen naturally.

Success happens because you are ready. Your prospect is ready. The opportunity is the right one, at the right time, in the right place, for the right reason, and you are the one with the key to the door on which he has been knocking.

Focus your energy on living up to your potential.
Work daily on creating a balance in your life that blends family, fun, fitness and finance into your routine. Listen to positive attitude tapes and read uplifting books. Fill your mind with harmony and all the best things of life. As you create an environment that welcomes success, you will naturally draw into your circle of influence people who are striving for the same things.

Success Reminders

- If you are having a bum week, you need to go to meetings to be re-energized and if you are on top of the world, someone in your group needs to see you at the meeting.

- Distributors and prospects duplicate what they see. If you are at a meeting and you want your prospect to learn the important stuff, take notes and watch them copy you.

- Recognize that some distributors with the brightest potential will never make it in this business. Some are just right down too smart. They have too much importance to be successful. They already have all the answers (which have nothing to do with what works) and you cannot tell them anything or teach them anything. Allow them to be - and move on.

- Create an environment within your group that supports the best in everybody. Celebrate the shade of the trees and the seats of the chairs but do not try to make something out of a person that is unnatural with who they are.

- Success happens because you are ready. Your prospect is ready. The opportunity is the right one, at the right time, in the right place, for the right reason, and you are the one with the key to the door on which he has been knocking.

Chapter 8:

Marketing Made Simple

A business thrives or crumbles on its marketing.
One of the great legendary geniuses of our time is the late
Buckminster Fuller who was the father of geodesic dome homes and
the inventor of the three-wheeled car - a vehicle so far before it is
time it was never embraced. His legend was the application of the
Dymaxion concept he left us, which promotes maximum perform-
ance with minimum materials or in other words, the ability to do
more with less.

If we were to apply his philosophy in marketing our small businesses, we would strive daily to find ways to maximize our time and
energy to reach more people without expending all our resources. In
addition, we would make every marketing dollar spent do the work
of three or four.

In order to do this it is necessary
to be clear about what you are
selling, and specify exactly how
you want people to participate in
your offer.

> *"Educated risks are the*
> *key to success. "*
> *–   William Olsten*

The Nitty-Gritty about Selling

Not too many people enjoy selling. Even fewer people enjoy being sold. Yet under every circumstance, you are either buying or selling.
You are buying into an idea, a set of beliefs or lack of, or you are trying to sell somebody on yours.

The difference between mediocre salespeople and great ones, is the great ones, are clear about what it is they are offering, and how far they will go to get it. And as an independent business owner you'd better know what you are offering, and offer it often—if you plan on surviving.

What Are You Selling?

Are you selling someone the chance to join you in business? Are you offering freedom from the daily grind of an 8 to 5? Are you marketing more time with the family or independence from a hated job? Are you passing out discounts on products everybody should be using? Does your product line fill some universal need?
Will those who join you be better off for knowing you and why?

Lifestyle Upgrade

Consider that most everyone is looking for an upgrade to his or her lifestyle. Learn to present your offer in a way that shows people a better way to live.

Even Bill Gates, a man with more money than the average person would consider an upgrade to better health, wealth or eternal youth - and the rest of the population is looking for the same solutions. Find a way to present your product, opportunity or ideas to people in an original and persuasive way. Then take your ad copy to the internet through your web page.

The internet is clouded with articles, advertisements and snippets of information that are funny, true, interesting and helpful. Learn to use these snippets to your advantage and put money in your pocket.

Know Your Offer

Know your offer backwards, forwards, and upside down. Know how you can help a prospect. Have your dream so clearly defined that you can inspire others to buy into your dream, making it a dream of their own.

Realize that most people's thinking is very chaotic. Most people have never articulated even to themselves what they want from life. If you can determine what somebody else wants, and then you can paint a picture and slide them into it, they are more likely to buy from you.

As you become a better presenter, you will learn how to use word pictures in your sales process. You will learn to create stories that include your prospect. And the better the picture you can create through words, the more accurate the image will be in other people's minds as they consider your deal.

Should you present your business to them in terms of prestige? More time with their family or more disposable leisure time?

Once you know what you are selling, and which approach you will use, it is easy to determine upcoming objections and resolve them before they arise.

There are numerous books that have been written on personality styles to determine which approach to use on whom but here are some simple guidelines:

Look visually at the person and their lifestyle. What do you see? Is this person polished and groomed? Drives a luxury car and wears only brand name or monogrammed clothing? He has a fancy wrist watch and carries a lizard skin daytimer?
Chances are, without really knowing him; you would take the prestige approach. It is obvious he is concerned what other people think about his choices.

Take the casual type who wears nice clothes but if you were to pay her a dollar she could not tell you the brand of the jeans she is wearing. She has a watch but it is strictly for telling time. And though she has a car, she is more concerned about reliable transportation than she is the latest model.
Chances are you would paint a practical picture for her where her joining your business could equal savings not prestige.

If you are not sure what type a person is (and sometimes it is hard to tell) listen to their conversation.
What do they talk about? Or gossip about? Are they bringing people down?
Chances are then, you would use on them the prestige approach, it seems they are concerned what others think of them, and so they bring others down to make themselves appear bigger than life.

How to Overcome Objections

There are only about eight or ten objections that ever come up in any sale.

- I don't have the time.
- I don't have the money.
- I don't see myself sponsoring people.
- I don't know anybody.
- I knew somebody who tried something like this and failed.
- This is too good to be true. It must be illegal.

Mastermind with a group of friends, who love you and want you to succeed in your business. Play the objections game where you write down all the objections you can think of, and then have somebody draw an objection out of a hat. Then go around the table and have each person answer that same objection with a different answer.

The winner of that round gets a point. And the person at the end of the game with the most points gets a free lunch and you all chip in.

Help each other learn the objections for your opportunity and create innovative ways to blend them into your presentation with finesse.

Before the prospect can ask you "how much does it cost?" You can say, "I bet you're wondering how much it costs?" Then get away from the price--call it an investment.

"Your total investment includes XYZ (then you go again over the benefits) is ONLY $19.95 a month." Then create a sense of urgency in a matter of fact way.

For example: "If we process your paperwork today, that only gives us six weeks to get 8 of your friends to that big regional meeting I was telling you about. Imagine the 10 of us on that Friday golfing before the rally."

Suddenly you are not promoting a business opportunity; you are promoting a lifestyle that includes the convention with his closest friends on a golf course. It is easier for a new prospect to imagine time with his friends than knocking on the doors of ten strangers and being laughed at for a new business he's starting.

> *"If you learn only methods,*
> *You will be tied to your methods,*
> *But if you learn the principles behind the methods,*
> *You can devise your own methods."*
> *- Ralph Waldo Emerson*

Marketing Through the Mail

Before you begin a marketing campaign, determine who your market is. It is not cool to waste resources by slinging your slogans in places they do not belong. Pick up a magazine, any magazine for that matter, and look at the advertisements inside. They are all along the same theme, addressed to a certain age group, social-class and income bracket.

A teen magazine for example would not advertise high-end notebook computers or $35,000 vehicles. Why? This is because a teenager is not likely to have the money to purchase those products and justify the cost of the marketing.

Targeting your audience will help justify the cost of marketing vs. your return on investment.

In order to know your market; ask yourself these five questions about your intended buyer:

1. Who will buy my product or opportunity?
This is where you determine your demographics i.e. age, gender, geographic location.

2. What are they buying?
This is not to be confused with what you are selling. You may be selling clothing; accessories or skin care products. Yet your customers may be buying fashion, youthful looks glamour and popularity. So in order to sell your wares, you need to make it look, smell, taste and feel like glamour, fashion, youth and popularity. Determine what you are selling in terms of *why* your customers will buy.

3. When will they buy?
Is your target audience on a purchase schedule? Do they get paid on Friday? If so, you will want to have your ads there on Thursday or Friday for those who impulse shop.

4. Where?
Where are they going to buy it? (From you, from a magazine, online, in a department store, directly from the manufacturer?)

5. Why?
Do your customers buy on need or emotion?

The answer to these questions will help determine an angle in which you can sell and get the most for your money.

How Many Ways Can You Market?

Marketing can be divided into many categories and is only limited by your imagination. Make a list of ways you could market or market your business. Write down every possibility even if it ridiculous. Here are some suggestions but feel free to add to the list.

- Billboards
- Sidewalk Sales
- Direct mail
- Telemarketing
- Teleconferencing
- Teleclasses
- Faxed Newsletters
- Faxed Advertisements
- Clearance Sales
- Articles in your local paper
- Brochures
- One sheet flyers
- Business Cards
- Ad Specialties
- Door Prizes
- Exclusive Reports

Billboards

Let's start with number one. While it probably is not realistic for most independent business owners to promote their business with a big billboard on the side of the road, a magnetic advertisement on the side of your car or truck might do the trick.

You might even consider a mini billboard in the form of a post card that you mail to all of your friends.

One of my colleagues and friend Jeff Davidson wrote a book called *Breathing Space* and then made 4 inch stickers that looked just like the cover of his book, He put them on every bill he paid, and every letter he sent. It was a mini billboard that brought him a wealth of exposure.

Sidewalk Sales

In the busy streets of New York City the merchants don't take sales for chance. They move their products outdoors on tables under bright colored awnings. They make a regular day of sales look like a celebration.

And while your products might be in a catalog or on the internet, you can still go outdoors and stir up some commotion. Have balloons and colored flags in front of your house. Put up a table with samples of the products you sell. Have a big sign announcing a drawing, give away prizes, and free soda to celebrate your business. Give your guests a brochure to take home or a flyer of the internet site you are promoting.

Direct Mail

Direct mail is incredibly expensive to the small business owner unless you learn the art of direct mail and then perfect it. Many books have been written on this very topic.

My two favorites are listed in the recommended reading list at the back of the book. If you are going to do direct mail, invest in a bulk mail permit available from your local post office. They run about $85 a year and allow you to mail at bulk mail prices.

For another $85 you can get a permit imprint which allows you to preprint postage on your mailer, then when you are ready to mail, you simply write the post office a check for the total amount of the postage. No more licking and sticking stamps.

Many post offices offer a free bulk mail training class so you can learn to sort your mail by zip codes, and regions.

Get a free postal mailing kit with instructions and regulations for bulk mail at your local post office. Check www.usps.gov for a post office near you.

Marketing on the Phone

Telemarketing is a great way to make money if you like rejection. We are trained to hang up on callers soliciting our time and attention not to mention our money. And while we don't like to be sold this way, there is a proper way to telemarket.

Never do it cold. By this I mean do not randomly call names out of the telephone book.

Once again, you want to target your market and work off referrals. If the person you are calling goes to your church, or is a friend of someone you know, the chances of him or her listening to you superb.

Teleconferencing

Imagine holding a business opportunity meeting in a different city every night? -- Without traveling?

Teleconferencing allows you to bring prospects to a live telephone call where an expert in your business support team can discuss the stairway to success. It is also very duplicable as your prospect can simply plug into the calls with his or her new prospects.

Teleclasses

Different from teleconferencing, teleclasses are ongoing lessons that often include workbooks and homework assignments. Teleclasses are prescheduled and prepaid in advance. And while there is no average fee for a teleclass, you will want to charge something that is affordable to most people. Around $20-$35 is about right.

You call your local telephone company and purchase a special multi-user telephone line for each session. Then at the designated time everyone, who has registered for the class, calls the telephone number and pays their own long distance charge to listen in. You keep the $20 or $35 dollars as a consulting fee.

It is customary to offer these clients a free newsletter via email or some other ongoing benefit for participating.

Marketing with the Fax

Newsletters if kept to one page are a great way to market your opportunity or products. Many computer software programs include the ability to broadcast fax meaning you compose the newsletter, program your computer to dial let's say 100 fax numbers and then you schedule a time for the computer to dial up your modem and begin sending your faxes.

The computer dials one telephone number at a time and then when there is a connection, it simply sends the fax.

When that fax is complete, it dials the next number on your list.

It is a great way to earn money if your computer is home dialing for dollars while you are out of the office.

* Sprint had a deal where as a small business if you signed up for their service, all calls you made on Friday's were free. Find a service

that offers a similar kind of deal and then send all your faxes out on Friday day so you are not paying long distance charges for every fax.

Also the length of your fax will determine how many seconds it takes to send the fax --and how much you pay per call.

Fax Advertisements

Faxed advertisements are more effective if disguised as a newsletter or article. And they tend to draw more attention of you have referrals of satisfied customers included.

Again, you will want to limit kind words about yourself and your company to a page. Most people will forgive you for sending a page, but if you take up eleven pages of their paper, toner and time they will ask to be removed from your list.

Be sure that you do leave contact information at the bottom of the ad so your reader can get back in touch with you to purchase, or get more information. Be sure to include your email address for those who want instant information, a fax back number (since all of these people have faxes) and of course a snail mail address in case somebody passes your ad along to someone in the dark ages with no technology to contact you.

Clearance Sales

If you have products, you purchased that are piling up in your house, or if you must buy $50 of something every month in order to qualify for a bonus, have a clearance sale.

While your focus would be to get your prospects and customers to purchase directly from the company so you make your commission, you can also introduce people to your business by giving them a one-time discount on your products. Chances are you will gain new customers who enjoy the products and then you can share with them the opportunity behind the products.

It is not wise to randomly "download at a discount" these products to people in your organization. This appears as if you have lost faith in the products and are "getting out" of the business.

If you are going to have a clearance sale, promote it properly for maximum benefit to build your business.
Some distributors have an annual "discount day" that they advertise everywhere and it attracts a lot of attention in their circles of influence. They serve cookies and punch and invite all of their friends to bring friends, then there is a mini business briefing, and everyone gets to leave with a bargain.

Get Published

There are daily, weekly, bi-weekly, tri-weekly, specialty papers in every city. Find out what is going on in your community and then figure out a way to work your products in around the community news.

Write an article about how it fits in and how people are using your products as a solution to a common problem. Be objective when you write the article, if it sounds too one sided, like you are the greatest thing since sliced bread, your article will be considered an advertisement and the paper will ask you to pay for your paper space.
Instead bill yourself as an expert and make yourself available for interviews. Other journalists may come and interview you. Radio stations are also looking for good talk show material and if you have valid points with an interesting twist, you will be interviewed.
Just like any other advertisement, make sure there is a way to contact you at the end of your article.

Brochures

It used to be that when you used the word brochure people would think of a tri-folded piece of paper with testimonials and great ad copy. Yes, that is what we are talking about plus much more. Brochures today can come in any form.

Terry, a local restaurant owner printed his menu on coffee mugs. The customer would get free coffee with a meal if they brought the mug in with them. This drew business in to the restaurant and then when they took their refill home they still had a copy of the menu on the mug.

Many multilevel companies have their brochures in audio format. They have found that people were more likely to listen to the opportunity while driving in their cars.

One group sells the business opportunity on tiny CD-ROM's the size of business cards. The innovative approach has captured the attention of millions.

Marketing with a Flyer

Brochures can also be one-sheet flyers. Flyers can be left on car and store windows; they can be faxed, mailed, or strategically placed on chairs before a big meeting begins.

The same rules apply to flyers as other forms of marketing; you do not just want to exhaust your energy and resources randomly passing out a bunch of fyers. Target your market. Then hone your marketing approach. Use persuasive ad copy and then be prepared to follow up. One note of caution here is if you do not have a plan to follow up, don't put out flyers. If someone calls your home office, you do not have an answering machine, and you are out prospecting you loose business. If someone goes to your web site and there is no form for them to fill out so you can get back in touch, you've simply wasted all that money on drawing prospects down a dead end street.

Marketing with a Business Card

The purpose of a business card is not just to give a prospect a way to get in touch with you - but to inspire them to get in touch with you.
Make sure your card is memorable.

Some people put their business photo on the card. While others include their mission statement on the back. Some folks include a discount off your first purchase and some simply leave a watt line where you can call 24 hours a day for a recorded message.

If you could only leave one sentence with the world, what would it be? And print that one sentence on the back of your card. Hopefully it provokes a response from the reader.

Be sure to include your email and website on your business card.

Ad Specialties

Ad specialties like any other form of marketing are as broad as your imagination. One distributor sent a targeted group of prospects an inexpensive rain poncho with a sticker attached it read: "Do you have money for a rainy day--or just this poncho?"
Then he included his telephone number.
The people who received it were blown away with his creativity and they of course picked up the telephone to hear more.

There are companies that have all kinds of gizmos for sale on which you can print your contact information.

Ink pens, hats, key chains, coffee mugs, clocks and more.
The object is not to overwhelm the prospect with advertisements but to catch their attention and get them to pick up the telephone and call.

Another distributor sent targeted groups of people a squeeze stress ball. On it was printed this: "The lack of money is the number one cause of stress. To cure the money problem call
1-800-Mon-E-Now. To cure the stress, squeeze this ball."

Door Prizes

Door prizes can be anything from candy to trinkets. The purpose of a door prize is to collect many prospect cards for a drawing and then to be introduced to the group, your name, business and opportunity. Then you go up to the front of the room and draw a name.
The real deal behind this is of course when you call back everyone from the meeting, they of course remember you because they saw you up at the front of the room when you were giving away the door prize.

If meetings you attend do not offer door prizes, bring your own. Make them nice generic gifts that anybody can receive and not too much about your company. The meeting planner will appreciate the give away and the fact that you were brief.

Exclusive Reports

Did you ever want to write a book? Why haven't you?
Statistics show us that most people want the prestige of being an author, without the trouble of sitting down to write. Perhaps you did

not think you had enough information to publish a whole book. So just publish a page or two.

One distributor wrote an incredible essay on the extremes people go to in order to prevent their telephones and power from being cut off when they lacked the money to pay their bills. He showed how much energy and resources were consumed trying to juggle payments around so the car and house weren't repossessed.
It was only one page. So he turned the page sideways, and folded it in half. It had a cover, followed by the two inside pages and then half of the back page.

He called it an "Exclusive Report of How to NEVER be Broke Again". He printed a price on the back cover of $6.95 for perceived value and then he gave them away to his distributors and prospects. (His duplicating costs were .06 cents per double-sided page.)
They all thought they were getting something for free, and he was educating them about the importance of working consistently day after day replacing old habits for new ones.

Who is the clever fool? The man who dreams or the man who wakes up and puts his dreams to action?

Success Reminders

- Make every marketing dollar you spend in your home-based business do the work of three or four.

- Everyone is looking for a way to upgrade his or her life. Learn to present your offer in a way that shows people a brighter way to live.

- Most people's thinking is very chaotic. Most people have never articulated even to themselves what they want from life. If you can determine what somebody else wants, and then you can paint a picture and slide them into it, they are more likely to buy from you.

- Before you begin an ad campaign, determine who your market is. You do not want to waste resources by slinging your slogans in places they do not belong. Targeting your audience will help justify the cost of marketing vs. your return on investment.

- If you could only leave one sentence with the world, what would it be? And that one sentence should be your slogan.

- Marketing is limited only to your imagination. The magic to successful marketing is in the mix. Consider trying various ways until you find ways that work well for you.

Chapter 9:

Internet Marketing

Email

Current marketing projections tell us that by the year 2005 there will be over one billion internet users. And how are you going to contact even a fraction of them if you are not on the internet?

In the last twenty-four months technology has changed so drastically, become so affordable, that even kids, teenagers, and retiree's are buying into the technology craze.

Computers are now sold with internet access and a modem. And you have a choice between a dozen internet service providers simply by clicking an icon and signing a monthly agreement.

Televisions can be connected to the internet using your screen as a monitor. You sit in your easy chair and with a wireless infrared keyboard, and can send and receive email and go web surfing.

The Internet for Beginners

Let's discuss the internet for beginners, because we all have to begin somewhere. In addition, there are thousands of ways to make money on the net either through email, e-newsletters, e-advertisements, e-commerce and websites. It is almost overwhelming. But let's start with your email address also known as a screen name.

If you don't have a website that is okay for now. At least get connected to the internet for the purpose of email. Email allows you to send and receive letters through your computer the same as you would a regular letter in the mail. The big difference is you don't print it out of your computer, put it in an envelope, write addresses on it or pay for postage. You can literally type a message and send it through the halls of the universe in just a few seconds.

In order to connect to the internet you need an internet service provider also known as an ISP. This is a company you pay monthly for the privilege of instant correspondence. Today (as this book goes to print) there are approximately 11000 internet service providers and you may have heard of some of the big ones like America Online, CompuServe, MSN, MCI, Prodigy, Quixnet, Earthlink and more.
The typical access fee is between $15.00-$30.00 per month for unlimited service. Some services charge more than others do and they offer a variety of options.

You pay for the service every month just like you would pay an access charges for a telephone number listed in your name. Only most Internet Service Providers encourage you to pay by automatic draft on your credit card.

And just like a telephone, an exclusive number or name identifies you. Most people use names because they are easier to remember than plain numbers and most Internet Service Providers allow you to pick the name you want to use.

So it is possible you could choose a name you like, or perhaps you would choose a humorous or silly name that has nothing to do with you and your business. One of the reasons people will use an online alias is the same reason people have unlisted telephone numbers. They want the pleasure of using the service without being identified.

Since you don't really know who is on the other end of a screen name, it is common business logic to treat all people who enter your electronic office with the same respect you would a friend.

Remember that it is easy to take your email and with one click, forward that message to one or many people. So, be careful of what you write and of course never write anything you do not want the world to read.

By the same token, if you write profound words that merit being forwarded, people (without your permission) will forward them to their friends and friends of friends, until your message travels through cyberspace and back to you.

Make all your writings worthy of that one forwarding click.

Follow all the rules of charisma when on the internet.

Speak no ill of your business team.

You may not have had the privilege of choosing a member of your support team. They may be a part of your network because someone in your group recruited them. However, they are an integral part of your business and as long as your network is in place, they will belong to your organization. Show them the same respect you would show your best friends.

Don't trash the company you represent.

If you do not like the company you work for, find a new one. If they pay you for your efforts, you owe it to them and their reputation to keep your feelings to yourself. There are times when it is appropriate to make suggestions, however making those suggestions out of context on line to a fellow distributor can dampen enthusiasm and kill the spirits of the people you are supposed to be inspiring.

Guard Your Online Reputation.

Refrain from forwarding dirty or demeaning jokes and stories. You can do better than that, and it's not classy.

Never dishonor those who honor you.

If somebody emails you, with a question, even if they are not in your direct pay line, still give them the courtesy they deserve. As you become a superstar, you will win the affection of people everywhere. Respect all people alike if you are to be counted among the greats.

Return messages as quickly as possible.

This one speaks for itself. Be prompt in returning mail so your prospects and friends know you are accessible and easy to communicate with.

> *"Always be polite and treat everybody right*
> *And in every way be affable and kind."*
> *– Folk Song*

If Somebody totally hates you

and sends you ugly mail, thank them for taking the time to contact you. People don't spend time sending hate mail, unless they somehow feel threatened by you, or you have done something irrational that was offensive to them. Treat it as constructive criticism and if you need to apologize, be the first to do so, but never toss back hate mail—with hate mail.

Before returning every email,

Ask yourself this:

If I were walking across a large stage in front of fifteen thousand distributors to receive an award, and as I walked across the stage, they broadcast this very email up on the overhead screens, would I be proud of myself or embarrassed?

How many E-mail boxes do you need?

It all depends on how organized you want to be and how you work your business. Some families share the maximum number of screen names also known as Pop names that a service provides. Some Internet Service Providers (ISP) provide you with three; four or seven screen names for one monthly internet access fee. Examples: America Online has a $21.95 unlimited access charge per month. And for that money, you can have as many as seven screen names.

When you register your own domain name some hosting packages provide you up to 25 screen names connected to your domain name.

And the purpose of having more than one is to streamline your business. For example, suppose you have five here is how you might allocate them for time saving purposes:

• Personal Use

- Prospects from Networking
- Distributor Inquiries
- Research
- Promotion or Marketing

Personal Use

This screen name is published in directories such as the neighbor-hood and church bulletins where friends or family can contact you about anything from community updates to other personal mail. If you have registered for any on line newsletters to be sent to you, they can send them to this address.

This box may not be urgent it is just a place where cousin Fred can forward stupid jokes and you can delete them when you get around to it, without sorting through precious business time to find out.

Prospects

This mailbox address is advertised on the bottom of your brochures or business cards targeted for prospects. When you visit this mail-box, you know everyone responding has met you personally from networking you have done.

Distributors

This mailbox is dedicated to the rest of your business support team and anyone else who might contact you on a regular basis. This mailbox is also the mailbox you use to send your weekly e-newsletters, snippets and important business updates. Keeping in touch with your organization is paramount so you will most likely check this box first so you can return messages, plan appointments and three way calls.

Research

Do not publish this address anywhere. You do not want anyone to know you are connected to this mailbox. You use this screen name when you are researching or cannot be interrupted while on the net.

Once your on-line marketing picks up, you will be inundated with Instant Messages (IM's) when you access a mailbox. In order to re-spect those responding (because you do not know who is on the other end of the message) you must be polite and answer all of the mail you receive. Having separate research mailbox or screen names allows you to move unrecognized by the general population through on-line databases of information, without being interrupted and al-lows you to keep your focus.

Promotion

This mailbox is connected to your marketing efforts and used to send your e-advertisements. This mail box sends press releases from a seemingly "outside source" telling others how great you are without it coming from your regular screen name that sends e-newsletters. This box can be assigned to a PR agency, a marketing rep for your company, or you can send the releases yourself.

Each screen name has it's own password so you can assign them out to those assisting you in your marketing efforts, or you can keep them all to yourself whichever you prefer. The purpose for several boxes is like having an electronic file cabinet with each mailbox rep-resenting a separate drawer. This way you only open the drawer of interest to you, without sifting through everything else.

What's In a Name?

On line everything. Your screen name is in essence a one-word advertisement. And you want to make sure that in sending out your advertisement or e-newsletter you always send it from the same address. Hopefully your screen name will represent your offer. Suppose your business opportunity is designed to catch the attention of those looking for additional income. Your screen name might be:

GetRich@MoneyLand.com

Even before I open your email, I know you have something to offer me regarding making extra money.

Let's assume that most people receive a mailbox a day of junk mail. This might include various internet offers, part-time business opportunities, Where to buy books, cameras, cars and more. Your offer is no different from all the other ones out there, until they recognize your screen name. By recognition, your e-mail can be quickly located and read in the mix of all the junk. If you are sending a regular advertisement or newsletter you will for sure want to use the same email address and the same subtitle or headline.

The One Line Sales Pitch

A subject line is a very short sales pitch. Your dynamic headline inspires the reader to open and read your mail. Use the same subject line or headline for each newsletter or advertisement you send.

If you send a weekly update to your organization, find a catchy phrase that you can use each week that creates brand recognition.

Many of my colleagues have weekly e-newsletters that are exclusive to their individual professions. One is called "Tim's Tips", while another has coined hers "A Word of Wellness". Wally sends me a weekly technology tip called "Monday Memo", and Sandra calls hers "Wednesday's Wisdom" and so on.

The purpose of using the same catchy phrase each week is simply recognition. I know without opening any of the e-newsletters mentioned above what to expect. There is a snippet of useful information followed with something inspirational, helpful or funny.

Even if I do not read Wally's Monday Memo- it makes me remember Wally. Wally for sure doesn't want to personally call or even contact every person, every week in his rolodex, but he is strategic enough to have found a way to make everyone in his rolodex think of him at least once a week.

His e-newsletter is the same as seeing him across the room and waving, "Hello there, Wally here"

Better yet, if I avoid reading it until the next day, I have simply thought of him again and have seen his electronic wave.

Imagine having your own weekly update or newsletter that positions you in front of you prospects and business support team.

This is effective for connecting with those in your organization. You want to be seen, but I am certain you don't want to have to call everyone in your group every day, or even every week.

With a broadcast email, you can be in touch with your entire organization with a couple dicks of the keyboard and presto; you are electronically waving to all of them on a regular basis. This also promotes them contacting you back. If they need your help, they simply hit reply and can send you questions.

Mass questions are also easy to answer. If you have a website, you can literally have a "Frequently Asked Questions" or (FAQ) page where you can direct traffic or you can cut and paste answers and send it to twenty inquiring minds at once.

Many newsletter software programs or webhosting companies include autoresponders that once you have written a message and have programmed the computer, you can run a filter on your incoming email.

This will search for preprogrammed words like "remove" if the incoming message has this word for example it will automatically remove the person from your email list.
It can also search for phrases like "More info" and if it sees this in the incoming message it will trigger a previously typed document of more information and send it to the person responding.

Such features allow you to communicate with your organization in a very productive way in a short amount of time with little effort, thus making the most of your marketing dollar.

Subject Lines that Get Opened

There's a catch to the one line sales pitch it cannot sound sales-y. Have you ever deleted an e-mail that was headed with a:
Get rich quick…
Hurry and open this…
Your last chance…
Never be fooled again…
It's happening!!!
An exclusive offer…
They are all gimmicks and some work better than others. Because we live in an era of skepticism, most people will delete anything that promises the world, the sun, the stars and the moon—without reading them.
Make certain your subject line for either your newsletter or promotion represents your offer without offending the reader.

Being sensitive to this, I share with you actual subject lines I have opened and why.

One read:
Jesus Wants You To Open This
Though I do not recommending using Jesus as a ploy to sell your wares, I did open it to see what it was Jesus was selling.

Another read:
Can You Refuse the Perfect Opportunity?
I opened this just to see what opportunity I might be refusing.

Per Your Request
This one usually gets opened because you are delivering information the reader has requested. Of course don't use it on someone, or a group of people who have not requested information, abusing this becomes a wicked ploy that will be viewed as a gimmick and tarnish your online reputation.

Rules for Understanding Women
I imagine this title was designed for both to male and female readers as women are in touch with understanding each other—and we men will forever wonder what just happened.

Age Erasers
Will catch the attention of anyone over twenty because of course; we are all in search of eternal youth.

Deleting this Can't Help You
This one promises help of some sort, and encourages action with curiosity.

Emails That Sell

Once you have a great screen name, a great headline and strong ad copy that will inspire your group and prospects to action, you can wrap it up with a reminder, slogan or a tag line.

A tag line is usually where people write the "sincerely" in a letter. Oh how boring. If large company can close with a parting thought, as a small company, you can too.

Pick a slogan that represents you, your mission or your vision. Use it regularly.

American Express for example used for several years "Don't leave home without it". It was at the end of all of their written promotions, correspondence and advertisements.

Coca-Cola used "Coke is it" and there's no question what is the "Choice of a New Generation" of course, Coke's competitor Pepsi.

So, create something memorable that stands out and sets you apart from all the other emails out there.
Usually your tag line will include (if you have one) your URL or your Web address. That would be your signature after your tag line.
It is helpful to always use the same tag line as well. It creates name recognition and gives people something consistent to count on.

The Reply Button

You have a responsibility when soliciting an audience that you give them what they are asking for. If someone hits reply to one of your email messages with a question regarding your business or products, be polite enough to respond as quickly as possible. Your professionalism is paramount even when you do not know who the person is on the other end of the line.

With email, it is easy now to connect from telephones across the country. Some cell phones allow you to answer email verbally while some pay phones in hotels and convention centers actually have keyboards attached to pay phones so you can send and receive email from the road.

Many distributors carry laptops and check their email remotely from hotel rooms. This is a very cost effective method of returning telephone calls. For the flat fee of a local domestic call (usually .75 cents to $1.00) you can log on in the city you are traveling. Connection fees range from $5.00- $9.00 when traveling internationally and the cost per minute varies. So check with your ISP before traveling abroad.

Some internet service providers have 800 or toll free numbers that allow you to connect to the internet when you are not in an area that provides local access within the continental US. This usually ranges from .05 cents per minute to .18 cents per minute depending on the carrier.

Rules vary from Internet Service Providers. Check with the one that you are using to determine the rules and regulations outlined in your contract. However, you will find it is usually more cost effective to return messages via email than snail mail or even telephone.

Write it Like You Mean it

Sending an e-mail is not the same as a telephone call or a meeting. It is better because it's faster and transcends time and geographical barriers. It is worse because it lacks the nuances of the spoken word and delivery gestures, leaving the message wide open to misinterpretation.

Be Brief

Have your offers no more than a few sentences long (10-30 seconds reading time is preferable.) Nobody wants to be locked into reading something that is long. So make sure when you write something, get right to the point.

Avoid run on sentences.

In addition, be sure to leave plenty of white space around your text so it is easy on the eyes. Computer screens are also more difficult to read from than a printed page, so consider that when sending e-ads or email.

Also, avoid colored text especially on the computer screen, it is very amateurish and hurts the eyes. Teenagers love it and that is about it.

Encoding and Attachments

Both attachments and encoding can create problems for the recipient and the network sending your message. They are a drain on the Internet because they increase the size of word files by one-third, while graphics and sound attachments can add many hundred thousand bytes to an email's size. This wastes the Internet's, and the recipients resources. The recipient must download larger files and there is no guarantee that encoded messages and attachments will be able to be decoded. It is best to just send your message, a few short sentences and type it in the message space instead of attaching it as a separate file.

Weekly Email Tip

So here's how you can keep in touch with a prospect, all your relatives, all your friends and business support team using technology.

Create a weekly e-newsletter. This can be informational, humorous, educational, or inspirational.

As you meet people collect and create a database of email addresses. Once a week send out your e-news to your entire list.

You certainly don't have the time to contact everyone on your list one-on-one. However, sending a weekly e-news is a consistent reminder of you and your business. Your reader has to think of you when they open their mail and they think of you even if they delete it. So you have in essence sent an electronic "hello."

If your prospect, family or friend wants to get back in touch with you, they simply hit "reply" on your email and you can correspond.

E-newsletters

Just as many companies have newsletters, the electronic newsletter is taking command over many small business who have learned that they can save printing and postage costs by delivering the same value in an electronic format.

There are companies who specialize in sorting lists of email addresses. There are also software programs that allow you to harvest email addresses from news groups. A news group is a group of people on the internet who join a chat room live to discuss a topic of mutual interest.

While this is a great way to capture the attention of lots of people rather inexpensively, there is also risk. Many Internet Service Providers have "no spamming" policies. If you get caught, they can boot you to Mars and take away your internet privileges. Your name is also put on a list of "spammers" and other internet service providers will not sell internet service to you.

The best way to catch the attention of like-minded people is to create a website and offer a free newsletter on it. People can register to receive your newsletter and then you are allowed to send them something of value in return. When I say value, I don't mean a well written advertisement, I mean an article, an informational snippet, and then the punch line is of course a reason to get back in touch with you.

The purpose of online newsletters is to inspire in others hope, unity and an upgrade to life. After you deliver value, then direct people to your website for more information, and an opportunity to take action on your offer.

E-advertisements
If you do advertise, do it in a tasteful, yet persuasive manner. The electronic advertisement is very similar to the electronic newsletter and if done properly, people won't even realize they are being sold. It is difficult to sell something without building confidence in your reader, so the e-advertisement works hand in hand with the e-mail and e-newsletters and your website. It is a combination of mediums all of which work.

> *"Marketing Magic is in the Mix." - Nido Qubein*

E-News vs. E-Ads
What is the difference between an E-Newsletter and an E-Advertisement?

An electronic newsletter is a short snippet of information or entertainment that you deliver as an added value to your friends and prospects. People like information, but don't like to be sold.

An advertisement is something for sale, either products, or an opportunity – or in essence something you get paid for to make a commission. It is important to separate your advertisements from your newsletters. Your newsletters will gain reader loyalty and generate the interest for your advertisements. When your reader requests information, you then send them your advertisement or refer them to your web page where the actual purchase can occur.

I recommend you NOT use the same screen name for both your e-newsletter and e-advertisement. Because you are most likely offering something in an ad that includes the suggestion of money or even a dollar sign.

Today's technology is so brilliant, that any internet user can place a filter against letters or "spam" aimed at selling a product or service. When the filter is activated, an autoresponder will automatically erase their email address from your mailing.
Then when you go to mail your next newsletter, that person will be gone from your list of prospects and or distributors.

Just like the e-news you will want your e-advertisement to include a progressive screen name that tells what you do.
If you small business promotes wellness and life balance, your screen name might be Longevity@freedom.com your screen name is also an advertisement that shows up in the readers box and is a determining factor in whether your message will be read or not.

Much like the subject line of the e-news, the subject line for an advertisement should be snappy. I recommend calling it an ad upfront.

Even with the most careful screening, your message may be unwelcome by some, so it's a good idea to let the recipient know that your offer is an advertisement before they open it. Your busy clients will appreciate it.

Example: "Life Balance Advertisement" for your subject line is more likely to be read by a busy person than "Special Offer."
Readers are tired of gimmicky sales approaches that promise to get rich quick or cure any ailment in a second. Be realistic in your approach and if you are selling something, say so.
Calling an advertisement an advertisement in the subject line begins to build loyalty even before the purchase has been considered.

Separate your Ads from News

If you don't separate the two, someone who doesn't like junk mail will ask to be deleted from your mailing list. Once they've been deleted they will not get your weekly e-news and will forget about you altogether. It is better to keep them as a prospect than lose them from your contact list.

Some mail programs allow you to keep separate mailing lists so you can separate the people out who don't want to be marketed to, but still want your regular informational tidbits of knowledge.
And while there are many mail programs on the market, here are some tips of what to look for in a good software program:

Installation and setup:

You want to search for a program that allows you to set up quickly and be running in a few hours. Features to look for include setup wizards; the ability to import settings, addresses, and mail from other programs; and support for multiple accounts and users.

Mail Composition:

Evaluate the program's options for creating and sending e-mail messages. Key features include support for HTML-formatted mail, spell checking, a wide array of send options such as recipient fields, delivery options, receipts, and priorities.

Address-Book Handling:

This category involves the program's address-book options, such as support for multiple address books, groups and mailing lists, and nicknames, and the ability to detach addresses from incoming and outgoing mail automatically.

Message Management:

As the volume of e-mail grows, this task becomes increasingly important. Factors to evaluate here include in-box design, folder handling, filter creation tools, and search capabilities.

Security:

Remember to weigh the program's support for encryption standards (S/MIME and PGP/MIME), encoding, password protection, and electronic signing.

Stand Alone E-news

Don't advertise in your enews.

Your web address at the bottom of your mailer is sufficient. Save adding more until you get to your advertisement. Also, many internet service providers now warn against hyperlinks that when clicked upon take you right to a web site.

Opening a site from an unfamiliar person could have links to viruses. Viruses can even attach themselves like magnets (unknown to you) to your email and be sent encoded in your hyperlinks.

This book was completely erased just days before going to press by opening an attachment from a friend. Of course it had to be reconstructed from scratch.

(Which reminds me to tell you to make absolutely certain you have back ups, and don't reinstall your back ups until you are completely certain the virus has been removed from your computer, your software and your external hard drives.)

Hyperlink Your Way to a Sale

If you include a hypertext link within the body of your message this is considered an advertisement. Automation systems that read "Spam" mail can detect a hypertext link and may block your e-mail from your readers. I suggest that you don't use hyperlinks in your regular submissions to your distributors unless they all know you.

A way around this is to use your web site address as your return mailing address. When they hit reply it will take them directly to your web site where they can browse, sign up for your free e-newsletter or contact you directly.

Or, you can leave your web address in your signature - at the end of your email or enewsletter.

The reader then can copy your web address and paste it in his or her internet connection and visit your site that way.

Once at your web page, they can order products and find out what else you have going. But avoid direct sales pitches from your e-newsletters mailbox at all costs. I am very passionate about this. Your readers will not consistently read your material if there is some gimmick attached or you are always trying to recruit them.

If your material is sound, and the reader is interested they will hit reply and ask you what you have for sale, or will follow your wisdom right to your website and in to your wallet.

Create E-News Reader Loyalty

Begin all your e-news with a question that jolts the reader to attention. You might issue some sort of challenge for the reader they can use today.

Valuable information, cutsie and humorous stories and stuff that makes you go "Hmmm", will get passed on and forwarded to families, friends, and other colleagues. Women especially, print things like this and pin them up at eye level in their offices.

Rate Your Sendings

Rate your sendings on a scale of 1 to 10. 10 might be a dynamic and thought provoking snippet. Only send 8, 9, and 10's. Information is a dime per three dozen now that we've approached the information age, and if you send anything below an 8 you will loose readers faster than you can say "You've Got Mail."

Remove my Name

If they do ask to be removed, remove them instantly.

They may later subscribe to your messages realizing how much they missed your weekly dose of ideas, but leave them with a positive memory of you and your company.

Whatever you do, don't start out your mailing with a header "If you want to be deleted from this mailing..." Saying so suggests to the reader that your material isn't worth reading in the first place and its condescending. Most readers are smart enough to hit reply if they want to be removed.

An autoresponder connected to your mailing, can search all incoming mail and if the word "remove" is anywhere in the message, it will automatically dismiss them from your list.

If you must say how to be removed you can have a snippet at the very end of your message. And make certain you place the removal instructions AFTER your signature and closing lines. It is NOT part of your message.

Be Creative

If somebody forwards you something on the internet, chances are it has been around the net a few times. I hate to be the one to shatter your hopes of belonging to an exclusive group that receives all the good stuff, but good stuff gets passed around to everyone, especially stuff that is unique or creative. So write your own good stuff instead of adding a header to somebody else's and get the credit you are due for your own ideas.

Authenticity goes a long way on the net and is one of the biggest secrets I can share with you in e-news success.

Using Dollar Figures

Never promise how much money someone is going to make from your offer. Such promises are not guaranteed and they hurt your credibility. Depending on the latest Federal Trade Commissions rules, it may be illegal as well.

Intelligent Readers

Assume your readers are intelligent but don't make them work too hard to understand your message. Be clear and concise about your message, avoiding fluff and unnecessary words. If you can think clearly, you should be able to write clearly, but you may need an editor to fine tune your writing for maximum results.

Jargon

Of course it is fun to impress your friends and relatives with fancy dictionary jargon. It is wise to avoid words that are exclusive to a particular group. In your e-notes be as general as possible to include everyone reading. You never know where it will be forwarded.

How Often Do You Send E-News?

You must send out a message regularly - Every 7-10 days. No Less. Otherwise people forget your screen name and they think your message is junk and they delete it without reading.

Many companies choose to send out a hard copy newsletter once a month or once a quarter. This is satisfactory if in hard copy format, because it gets kicked around the clients office or pinned up on a bulletin and is visually seen more frequently than an e-mail.

On e-mail, you basically get one chance to either be read or deleted. So take the time to send it often enough that you won't be forgotten.

Don't send it so often that you get in their way. Daily would be pestful to most busy clients and customers. Weekly is enough if your information is sound. They will look forward to receiving it and will make a habit of reading your electronic newsletter or note when it arrives.

If your electronic news replaces a slick glossy hard copy you are currently sending, you can simply split your regular newsletter up into four parts and send out one part each week.

This way, you have spent no more time in preparation of your newsletter, you have sacrificed nothing, and have saved the printing, labels, mail sorting, mail service, and postage costs. Not to mention that your electronic newsletter or advertisement arrives two to three days quicker than a snail-mail version.

Small printers are going to start hating me for taking their business to the internet, but you can save a ton of money in your small business if you switch from hard copy to electronic copy.
Soon, we will all be sending brochures, newsletters, advertisements and press releases over the net.
Don't get left behind.

If you don't have a computer and you aren't on line, run to your nearest computer store and invest in a computer.

Just to get on the internet, there are now other options than computers, the key to remember though is a computer does what a computer was designed to do, including the operation of specific software, database housing of your contact information, back up capabilities, mail merge capacity, broadcast faxing, broadcast emailing, web access, accounting software, the big five: Microsoft's Power-Point™, Access™, Word™, Excel™,and Outlook™.

Many of the new entertainment devices that include internet access do not have CD ROM capabilities so you can not install new software and they don't have the capacity to hold contact management software which is crucial to you keeping track of your business support team.

The days of recipe-card holders with handwritten names and phone numbers are a thing of the past.

The cost you might invest in a computer will most likely offset your newsletter printing costs within the year.

You can use your computer for lots more things than just sending out weekly newsletters too. Juxtapose the cost of a computer with the current cost of marketing and see how much of your advertising dollars could save you in on-line marketing.

Include Your Prospects

Everybody wants to belong to something bigger than themselves. That is one of the biggest reasons network marketing is so successful. To capitalize on that very issue many companies insist on a printed newsletter so they can print photos of best customers. This is a wonderful idea and also builds in a networking business, distributor goodwill and loyalty, however, if you are printing photos of your distributors and prospects in your hard copy newsletter, consider putting those photos on your web page on a "Superstars" sheet. This will generate lots of traffic, as your organization will return regularly to your site to see their own face. They will bring with them family and friends who in turn see your other offers for sale and links to various web sites.

Although a hard copy newsletter has value, your distributors and prospects can forward your web page address to friends and clients everywhere opposed to having one hard copy to carry around in their brief case.

Best Day of the Week to E-News?

The best time to send your message is a week-night.

If it hits your client or prospects mailbox Friday, Sat, or Sunday night, chances are it will be read at home while the TV is going. Typically, no actions are taken on weekend mail. I do not really know why, it has just been my experience that weekend mail for either e-newsletters or advertisements is a waste of time.

On the other hand, if your reader has a desk job where they sit all day playing on the computer with nothing better to do, they will most likely pay attention to your e-news or ad, and print it out, hang it on the wall and/or forward it on to their friends.

Effective Advertisements

Keep your initial offer short. Five or six sentences long and don't give the reader enough information to buy at first glance. Most people buy based on need or emotion and it is rare that you will elicit a need, offer a solution and close a sale all at once.

Have a two-part ad.

The first part is snappy and hits on a need or emotion. If they are interested, they can hit reply and type in a key word. When you see the keyword in your mail-box, you simply send part two of the ad (or have an autoresponder send it) that has all of your credibility and how to purchase information.

Once you have the attention of your reader, and they hit reply for additional information from you, you have the sale. By responding to you, they are admitting you have touched a nerve and they are interested, and you have them interacting with you. Once you have them interacting, it is easier for them to send you payment.

Attention Span of Consumers

Keep your message short and simple.

The same rule applies to the e-note and the advertisement. If you are sending your message to clients, chances are they will read it at work.

If your message is too long (Anything beyond 10-30 seconds worth of reading, it might get saved to flashmail or a "I'll read it later mail box", then never revisited.) Don't run the risk of sending too much information at once.

Remember we live in a bullet point society that is picking up pace. This keeps the readers attention, and saves bandwidth.

For those who travel, downloading large files and attachments can become costly. Some overseas internet service providers charge an international access fee to collect email in their country.

When you keep your message short and to the point, you show your customers and prospects that you are respectful of their time.

The less you say, the more likely it is for a prospect to read your offer which means your every word must be calculated and delivered with pizzazz.

Send the Right Stuff

Is your offer targeted to an association, corporation or other targeted groups? The more you know about each, the better, because when you send a perfectly crafted promotional e-mail, it has to be as customized as possible. You will want to use the lingo that the group or association uses. And if you know that the organization to which you are mailing has an upcoming event, you can wrap your time sensitive offer around it.

Some mail programs now allow you to mail merge the contacts name and city in your email to them. This makes them feel as if they were getting a personal invitation to purchase directly from you.

Targeted E-mail

Internet Service Providers offer their customers the ability to sign up for specific information to be sent at specific times when they are in buying mode. The Internet Service Providers will sell you a list of targeted names, which take the guesswork out of spam or junk mail.

Individuals choose to subscribe or unsubscribe to any series of offers and today's powerful data-gathering technologies allow us to define our information profiles in intricate detail.

Lose Friends and Irritate People

Just throw names in your file without checking for duplicates. Harvest names out of news groups and spam people with unsolicited emails.

If you attend enough business opportunity meetings, write enough articles, or become a regular at local community meetings, you will run into folks who subscribe to your mailing more than once. Adding them to your list without sorting them causes irritation on the reader when they open their mail box and find your message four-teen times.

Right now there are several email software programs that offer name cleaning from your lists. You simply run a sort before each broadcast emailing and the program cleans up your list for you so there are no duplicates or inaccurate addresses.

Track Your Success

Using the Internet for marketing is still unproven and unreliable, and today it is a low-risk proposition, so we marketers are free to ex-periment. It is not hard to recover from mistakes and update one's web site or marketing approach. There is however, talk of charging a postage fee to internet postings, so now is the time to discover what is worth paying for and what isn't. Keeping good records is useful for more things than just paying taxes.

Email newsletter success is affected by two factors:

Factor One: Easy access to the Net.
If you travel frequently and you are the one sending your weekly e-newsletter or other offer, you must have a mobile on-line connection. If you have a laptop and a modem you can essentially send your messages from any hotel room. If you don't have access to a laptop or notebook computer, you can take discs with you and connect in the business center at a hotel, (open usually from 6:00am-9:00pm) or at a Kinko's found in most US cities (open 24hrs.)

Some mailing software programs have a scheduler attached that al-lows you to program your computer to start up at a specific time and send your message. The ideal way to do your internet marketing of course is all automatic. Check around before making a purchase and determine what your needs are, and then invest in the software and equipment that will perform your requirements.

Note: Many software programs that promote your business are also tax deductible.

Factor Two: Your ability to complete projects on time, consistently. If you are a chronic procrastinator, make yourself a calendar and place your e-news and e-advertisement dates on it. Marketing time needs to be blocked out just like appointments with prospects.

Your readers can't read what you don't send, and your buyers can't buy what they don't know is for sale.

Marketing either through traditional or unconventional methods comes down to four basics elements that when combined create success:

1. Analyze everything.
2. Question everything.
3. Repeat what works.
4. Make the process duplicable.

Bulk Email

Bulk email can be considered to mean many things. And the rules of bulk e-mail are changing rapidly. It used to be that you could send bulk e-mail in mass to people in blind carbon copy format.

Blind carbon copy means the reader can only see his name at the top of the letter, not all the names of the other hundreds of people who received the same message.

The purpose of blind carbon copy is to eliminate the possibility of every reader receiving a copy of your entire mailing list. Exposing your entire mailing list allows anyone on the list, to copy the names of other recipients and send them unsolicited mail.

In September 1999, the Federal Trade Commission outlawed bulk email also known as "spam." Check with your local internet service provider for current rules and restrictions. Then check the resource guide at the back of this book for software programs that assist you in your online marketing.

Success Reminders

- Remember that it is easy with one click of a mouse to forward your message to another person --or many people. Make all your writings worthy of that one click.

- Imagine having your own weekly update or newsletter that positions you in front of you prospects and business support team.

- This is effective for connecting with those in your organization. It allows you to be seen without personally connecting with everyone in your group.

- You have a responsibility when soliciting an audience, to give them what they are asking for. If someone hits reply to one of your email messages with a question regarding your business or products, be polite enough to respond as quickly as possible.

- An electronic newsletter is a short snippet of information or entertainment delivered to your clients and prospects. People like information, but typically do not like to be sold.

- An advertisement is something for sale, either products, or an opportunity – or in essence something you get paid for or make a commission from.

- Begin all your e-newsletters with a question that jolts the reader to their attention. Or start out your message with an inspirational story. You might have some sort of challenge for the reader they can use or implement today.

- Have back ups, and in the event you are infected with a computer virus don't reinstall your back ups until you are completely certain the virus has been removed from your computer, your software and your external hard drives.

- Marketing either through traditional or unconventional routes comes down to four basics that combined create success:
1. Analyze everything,
2. Question everything,
3. Repeat what works,
4. Make the process duplicatable.

Chapter 10:

Marketing on the Web

Web Pages

Marketing is clearly changing. Look around you, television ads are now designed to look like web pages. Web addresses are posted on vehicles, billboards and paper bags from your local fast food chains. Everybody is touting their web address on all of their printed material. How about you? Do you have a web address?

If you haven't invested in one because you can't justify the price, ask yourself this: can I afford for my friends and prospects to look me up on the world wide web and find someone else using my name.com, or my company name. com?

> "The greatest profits are made on a great volume of small profit."
> - Mary Kay Ash

When you reserve your name.com or your company.com this is called a domain name. And you can reserve yours today for two years for as little as $70 dollars at www.reserveme.com. They will send you a bill or you can pay on line with a credit card. Then they bill you $35 a year after the first two years, every year as long as you keep the domain name.

Think of it as a world-wide investment because there can only be one you.com or one you.net.

Another approach that is winning worldwide popularity is networking companies allowing their distributors to tag along as a distributor@TheMainDomainName.com.
The benefit of tagging along with a bigger company of course is the credibility factor. Suddenly in just a screen name you have aligned yourself with the successful track record of a company five or ten years old.

Although it is difficult to know the age or type of person on the other end of an email screen name, it is important to your on line marketing to understand a few things about an internet user.
First of all, they know how to read and write (or type for that matter.) Chances are they own the computer they are using, are paying for their monthly internet service with a credit card and have most likely made a few buying decisions on line as well.

There are software programs available on the market that link a status report to your web site to help determine what words (from search engines) were used to find your site. The status report allows you to refine your target audience.

You can run a filter through some websites that allow you to offer a special bonus or premium products to a specific audience and block out the rest.

Web Catalogs

Catalogs are moving to the World Wide Web. Instead of a distributor ordering and passing out catalogs to their prospects as was customary in the past with companies such as Amway, Avon, Sunrider,

Tupperware, Candle Lite, and others, catalogs can now be displayed as web pages. Some are even pass code protected with a distributor number.

The benefits of this are three fold:
1. Catalogs are expensive to produce and are time sensitive. Once a catalog is printed, there is a concern if the manufacturer of the product is still able to offer the products at the advertised price or selection.
2. Web pages are expensive to produce also, and are even more time sensitive than catalogs because they can be updated and changed instantly. Suppose you have a product advertised on your web site and suddenly it becomes unavailable to the masses. Your web master can remove the product from the line up and within minutes the advertisement is erased from the electronic catalog.
3. You can give out your distributor number to friends to use when they visit your company's website. If they purchase products, using your number as the pass code a commission can be traced back to you and you get the credit for the sale.

Marketing on the internet is a combination of old and new marketing. The old way is paper based: catalogs, brochures, business cards, direct mail and faxes. The new way includes all of the above in electronic format. If you choose to still use paper marketing, design it in a way that drives traffic to your e-business.

• Print your web address and email on all your promotional material.

• Include your web address in the return address section on every bill you pay and every letter you send.

- Include your web address with your signature. Every time your sign your name to a check, credit card slip, or letter write your web address.

- Direct traffic from your telephone answering machine to your website.

- Include your web address with every email you send. This way your prospect can learn more about you and your company.

- Don't risk losing a prospect who calls you. On your telephone answering machine, leave your web address and email as an alternative way of reaching you.

- Buy a custom rubber stamp that has your email screen name and web address on them. Use it on all company literature and brochures you pass out. Because the internet is world wide, regardless of where you move, it will not become outdated like a street address or a home telephone. Even if you move across the country, you can still keep the same email and the same website address.

Be Available when You're Not

A website is a very economical way to let your organization get in touch with you when you are "not there". From just about any computer, you can tap into a web page and pull up success stories of what is working in your organization.

- Link your web page to the web pages of other distributors in your group who represent various backgrounds and income levels.

• Highlight your superstars on your web page in a recruiters hall of fame. Have their picture and a detailed description of their story and how they became so successful. Of course those highlighted will tell all their friends and family about the write up and publicity you gave them. All of their friends and relatives will go to your website to view the recruiters hall of fame, while other distributors in your group will recruit like crazy to reach the coveted position of publicity on your web site.

Some organizations have their own group web site that is accessed simply with a distributor or distributor number. Inside that website information can be accessed about all the upcoming events, product specials and so on. Before you go creating your own web page or web site, check with your business support team to see if your organization offers such a web site that you can simply join for a few bucks a month.

To be successful in MLM, learn to be visible. Be seen. Be available to those who admire and respect you. Learn to be there even when you aren't there.

Use of Graphics

Reuse your graphics on different pages of your web site. Browsers locate and read the photo or graphic only once and then store it for the remainder of the session. Every subsequent time the browser encounters that same graphic, the computer instantly pops it back onto the page without reloading it.

Now Picture This

Digital cameras are now popular with high quality resolution. With auto flash, auto focus and auto centering, anyone can aim, click and presto—have a photo ready to email to family and friends.

Film can be stored on a disc or CD instead of the old fashioned way of taking it to the developers and waiting a few weeks for the photos to be mailed back to you.

Many photo developers now offer email service for photo developing for people who do not have digital cameras and scanners. You simply use your regular camera to take photos like you always did, and when you take them to the developer, you request email service.

Your photos are delivered to you online and you can view them, store them to a computerized photo album, attach them to an email or uplink them to your web page.

Think of the many applications where you could motivate your support team by sending them pictures of the world as you travel.

Banners

The top of the page is most important part of your web page. It is like the headline of a newspaper and is called a banner.

A browser like Microsoft Internet Explorer or Netscape is used to translate your web page from computer code to words and pictures that are easy to understand. This translation process is called "loading." You might even have to wait a few seconds for a browser to load a page.

So it is important to have a cool banner or catchy headline that your prospects can read while they are waiting those few seconds for your page to load.

Use Search Engines

There are over 400 search engines that allow you to fill out a registration form on line for free to be listed with them. Listing your website with the search engines means that you have a keyword or series of keywords you register. For example: *Independent Business Owner* might be three words you list with the various search engines.

Here's how it works. Lets suppose that Karen Peterson, who lives in New Jersey goes to her home computer and signs on to the internet. She goes to the World Wide Web and types in a search for the words *Independent Business Owner.* The search engines will search for all the web pages that include those words and then pull up on her screen a menu of options she can choose from.

Now it is possible that you may not be the only one who has registered those three words. So even if the search engines pull up your information, they might pull up the web pages in the menu for 50,000 other web sites that include the same three words.

Don't count on the search engines to drive traffic to your site. You have to do other promotion as well. You will want to put your web site address as discussed earlier by printing your web address on your business cards, brochures, flyers, magnetic billboard on your vehicle. Make sure your email address and web address are left on your telephone answering service or machine and are also listed on regular postal mail in the return mailing section.

Scavengers

There are people in cyberland who thrive on free stuff. It doesn't matter what it is, as long as it is free.

Make certain when you design your web site you include lots of free stuff, and let your prospects download it from your website. Have a "free stuff" section with articles and snippets they can quote and use.

Offer all of your free stuff on the web so that you are not paying the costs of packaging and shipping stuff out through regular mail.

Despite the hype, most companies are still in the earliest stages of e-business and lack effective e-business strategies, according to research groups. Companies see their friends and competitors on the internet so they create their own web sites but they really don't know what they are doing.

Success Reminders

- The greatest profits are made on a great volume of small profit.

- Consider registering your name.com as an investment. Regardless of what you do for the rest of your life, you can promote it on your web site.

- If you choose to still use paper marketing, design it in a way that drives traffic to your web page and emails.

- Web sites are less expensive in the long run to print than catalogs or brochures and can be updated as necessary.

- Link your web page to the web pages of other distributor's in your group who represent various backgrounds and income levels.

- The headline or banner of your web page is the most important part of the page because people browsing will determine within seconds whether to hang out or move on to another page.

- Print your web address and email on all your promotional material.

- Include your web address in the return address section on every bill you pay and every letter you send.

- Include your web address with your signature. Every time your sign your name to a check, credit card slip, or letter write your web address.

- Direct traffic from your telephone answering machine to your website.

- Include your web address with every email you send. This way your prospect can learn more about you and your company.

- Don't risk losing a prospect who calls you. On your telephone answering machine, leave your web address and email as an alternative way of reaching you.

- A website is a very economical way to let your distributor's get in touch with you when you are "not there". If you don't have one, it is time to reconsider.

Chapter 11:

How to Write Great Ad Copy

Great ad copy is crucial when you are sending an email to your downline or prospects, because your words will generate activity within your organization.

If writing is not a strength for you, find someone within your group who can help you write emails, e-news and web pages, until you get the hang of it.

Get Someone to Help You

Do you have a persuasive friend who is constantly telling you about the latest, greatest whatever? Soon they have purchased into the idea and have your money tied up in it too?

Hang out a little longer with these kinds of friends, they are really salespeople in disguise with the power of suggestion on their side.

Have them pretend like they are selling your product and take notes. Use the words they use. Try to see your product or service from their eyes. Why are they so enthusiastic about it?

Keep Your Presentation Simple

When someone else explains your products or business opportunity, they will most likely not be as eloquent as you. They will not know where your products are manufactured, or how many years the business has been existence, they will not remember if it was listed on Inc Magazines top 500 list, or model numbers of products for sale. What they will remember is what it does, and how it applies to them.

Sell What People Are Buying

Are you selling your opportunity in such a way that the guy listening to your deal gets so excited, that he runs out and tells all his friends and family? If not, change what you are selling.

You will break into the big money in this business when your customers start selling to their friends, what you sold to him.

One of the top retailers in a water filter MLM realized early on in her career that people were not buying water filters. The public did not understand the benefits of granular activated carbon or about the iron, sulfur, lead, chlorine or manganese in the municipal city water systems.

She quickly changed her approach and instead of selling water filters, she sold the exact same product, but marketed it as a "do-it-yourself Bottled Water Kit"

She cut all the technical details out of the presentation, simply attached the demo unit to kitchen sinks across the country and then asked her customers for a jug, which she then proceeded to fill with water. "See how easy?" she commented all the way to the bank. It was so easy it was duplicable and she filled the positions in her organization like she filled water jugs.

Surf the Web

If you find yourself for more than a few seconds on a web site, stop and look around. What do you see? Are the colors pleasing to the eye? Is the layout easy to use? Is there a banner or a sidebar with options that take you easily where you want to go for more information?

If there are questions on the website, do you find yourself answering them?

Bookmark these sites so you can return later to do a detailed study or better yet, keep a list of your coolest top 100 web sites.

Can you use some of these same successful elements in creating an advertisement or web site for yourself?

Analyze Junk Mail

Although email and web sites are a wave of the future, do not forget the time proven techniques of regular old postal snail mail. Direct mail through the postal system has made many a millionaire and there are books in my recommended reading list that will give you some great ideas you can use to promote your new opportunity. Here is one:

Do the three-second quiz. If you look a piece of junk mail longer than three seconds there is obviously something about it that is catching your attention.

The most consideration the bulk of snail mail gets today, is in the hands of the postmaster himself when he is trying to read the address. Lots of it gets tossed in the trash without ever being opened.

So, if an article or mail piece catches your eye examine it.

Is the envelope a funny shape or color? Does it have a bright colored sticker on the front of it? Are the words on the outside of the mailer persuasive enough that you open it? Or have they used the plain white envelope, hand written, hand stamped curiosity approach?

Ask yourself, what makes you open some mail, while you throw the rest away?

Keep a box of "best junk mail" to use when creating your own advertisements.

Use High Impact Words

The art is to blend them in with normal phrases you use. It is not cute or persuasive to run around yacking at people like you are Shakespeare. You want to sound like you know what you are talking about with a ten-dollar word tossed in here and there for impact.

Listen for Catchy Words

Catchy words are also used in the selling process on purpose to inspire a purchase. Captivating words are very successful in brochures, on web pages, on flyers, in newspaper ads and in television commercials.

Some night when you're up late and can't sleep, turn on the TV and pay attention to late night infomercials. You will be surprised at the kinds of empowering phrases that make it easy to invest $69.95 a month, in four automatic installments. Or grab any newspaper and a marker and circle all the catchy headlines and sales phrases. Make your own list of catchy words or add to the list below.

Revisited	Lively Market	Will Power
Under Priced	Specialized	Endurance
Just In Time	Nostalgic	Liberated
Profitable	Decision	Focus

Stardom

Flex

Portfolio

Surging

Comprehensive

On

Gaining

Heritage

Slash

Concept

Mainstream

Unlock

School of Thought

Preppie

Up Scale

Economic Needs

Spotlight

Remarkable

Critical

A sampler of

Show Me

Innovative

Epidemic

Next Frontier

Boom

Merit

Competitive

Breakthrough

Block Busting

Envision

Novel

Promising

Challenging

Flourishes

Nest Egg

Round Table

Gut Feeling

Monitor

Masterpiece

New

Brave

Obsession

Starter Kit

Late Breaking

Billboard

Timely

Avoiding

Word of Mouth

Soar

Mania

Alarming

Tech Revolution

Hybrid

Renaissance Spirit

Compromise

Opportunity

Reviewing

Rewards

Fundamental

Edge

Monumental

Investor

Exercising

Economical

A gallery of

Test Drive

Cost Shifting

Energy

Enterprising

Overrated

Savvy

Reminiscent

Ultimate

Distinguished

Bonanza

Effective

News Wire

Tenacity

Lively

Sure Fire

Daring

Forecast

Shrewd

Crucial

Top Dog

Exploit

Foothold

Last Minute

Revolution

Survival

Bottom Line

Technology

Launching

Philosophy

Formula

Alert

Improved

High Yield

Lifeblood

High Tech	Value Line	Zingers
Insatiable	Property	Successful
Imagination	Switch	Hot
Ownership	Traces	Growth
Excitement	Skill	Hot off the Press
Security for your dollar		Views
90 days same as cash	Complete	Generic

Use Compelling Headlines

If you have ever wondered the power of headlines think of the tabloids you see in the checkout line at the grocery store. The headlines are constructed in such a way they generate just enough curiosity you want to pick up the paper and read more.

Many magazines and books are sold on headline, and title alone. There seems to be some sort of promise that engages the reader.

Learn this lesson from the daily news, junk mail advertisements, magazine covers, tabloids, billboards and websites. Snatch the attention of your prospects and downline with compelling ad copy in all your emails, e-news, web pages and other correspondence.

Sell like You Buy

Think back to the last time that you bought a car. Did the salesperson use words that made you proud as a potential owner of that car? Did he use a phrase or line to close the sale that created a sense of urgency?

Did he make you feel wise for making an informed and educated decision?

Did he give you his own opinion to add credibility? Did he tell you which of the models they have for sale he was personally driving?

Consumer statistics show us that 30% of people buy or act on impulse. Thirty percent! Are you catering to that thirty percent of people who make decisions spontaneously? Do you resolve common objections right up front?

Does your offer look logical, sound logical and feel logical to someone who is qualified to make a buying decision about your business or product line today?

Or do you assume that all of your prospects need to take six weeks to make a decision because Aaron down the street took that long to decide if your offer was conducive to his lifestyle.

Keep a File of Great Ad Copy

I actually keep mine in a file on my laptop so I can fire off an advertisement, newsletter or inspirational broadcast email or fax in a pinch.

Keep a computerized file or a big envelope of great ad copy you can borrow from when writing an impressive sales piece. Remember that you are always selling something to somebody, whether it is a position in your business, or an idea, or a rumor. And you always want to sound like you have the best deal going. If you keep a file, you will never be short of words.

Every Email is An Advertisement

As you practice refining the art of writing, your skills will increase. Moreover, the best way to become great is to practice. Consciously decide to give every email your best writing efforts. Take care to always choose the best words possible. If you need a stronger word to emphasize a point, take the time to stop and look it up. Soon you will have all kinds of electrifying words running off the tip of your tongue.

Set Aside Marketing Time

Marketing is one of, if not the most important element of your business. If you have the greatest deal in the world but nobody knows about it, your business will eventually die. You have to share your message with a considerable number of people if you are to be a success in any endeavor. If people are not buying, you are not making any money. In addition, without money, how will you pay your bills?

In order to maximize your time and efforts, it is wise to use vehicles that take your message to the maximum number of places, in the shortest amount of time, for the least amount of money. Your words, e-newsletters, e-mails, e-advertisements will go places you as a person will never go. You could not possibly go all the places and say all the words to all the people in the length of time it takes to send your message around the world instantly via the internet.

Learn to use the internet to spread your words of hope and profitability. Mark your calendar in advance when you will take time to market your business. If you do not schedule it out in advance, it is easy to fill that prime marketing time with endless other tasks.

Review, Review, Review

Although your advertisement or message might make perfect sense to you, it might be confusing to another person. Have you ever seen an ad that made you crunch your nose up and go huh? Or perhaps you have heard a radio commercial and you simply did not "get it."

I assume you are expecting more impact from your marketing – so remember to prepare your words carefully. If you give regular sales pitches vocally, tape record it and listen to it over and over again.

Listen at different times of the day when you are in different moods and your energy is at a different level than when you recorded it. Does it make as much sense when you are tired as when you are awake?

If your pitch is in writing, put it aside for a few days without looking at it and then revisit it again. The smallest changes will be easy to spot or you might think of a better way to say what you previously said.

Update Regularly

It continually amazes me how many professionals pass out business cards that have old telephone numbers on them. Then they cross out one number and hand write in another. Talk about tacky. Or they have business cards that have a telephone number but no email address. Worse yet, some folks do have their web sites printed on their business cards and when you get to their site, lo and behold, six month old information is posted up there about some upcoming (passed) business opportunity meeting.

Update your marketing info, websites, business cards, and flyers often and keep your materials fresh. If you are in business and you are demanding attention from a prospect, they expect and deserve your very best.

Become a Twistologist

Have you ever seen the award winning Absolute Vodka advertisements? Coffee table books have been created just with their ads alone. They took their product and then twisted it every way possible, targeting as many audiences, in a variety of age groups, for as many occasions as possible.

You want to do the same with your ads whether they are print ads, electronic ads, verbal ads and so on.

Include All Age Groups

Most businesses are not age sensitive and yours shouldn't be either. Include stories in your presentations that seniors, juniors, youth and everyone in between can identify with. If you have print ads try to have a nice variety of pictures that include the maximum range of people. You do not want to appear as if you are catering to a particular age group or ignoring a generation of potential distributor's.

Be Sensitive

Be sensitive to gender, political, religious and social groups.
The object here is to use tact and try not to offend anyone. Take care not to blatantly leave anyone out of your circle of influence. If your message is good, it will be passed around the globe through the power of networking in your organization. If you do your job correctly, people will talk about you and the inspiration you or your written words have been--and they will want to participate in your group. Try to inspire, not alienate.

Create a Mastermind Group

Find a small group of friends who share your marketing interests and mastermind with them every month or so. Share your objectives and get opinions from those who are equally enthusiastic about your business.

Building your own marketing campaign can be fun if you do it yourself, and at the same time can be a very slow and expensive learning process. If you choose to do it yourself, it will require tenacity on your part and regular practice.
Keep a marketing journal/file with all of the things you have tried. Note what worked and what did not.

If you find something that works, share it with your business support team. If it easy to duplicate, soon you will have an army of people earning money with your tactics that will increase your net in unlimited revenues.

Success Reminders

Great ad copy is crucial when you are sending an email to your organization because your words will generate activity. Also consider that the written word will go farther than your voice will ever go because in cyberspace, your message can be forwarded thousands of times in a matter of minutes.

- If writing is not your specialty, solicit help from a creative friend who knows how to write.

- Sell what people are buying. If you are selling an ordinary product, become a twistologist and create a new use for it.

- Surf the web and find cool web sites and cool pictures. Make notes of what catches your attention.

- Analyze Junk Mail and keep a copy of great ads. Learn from others who have spent careers inspiring a purchase.

- Use compelling words and headlines in all of your advertising, emails and websites.

- Set aside marketing time with a mastermind group. Ask for and be open to honest feedback. Now is not the time to wear your sensitivities on your shoulders. Good marketing advice is worth it's weight in gold.

- Update and review all your materials regularly.

- As you practice refining the art of writing, your skills will increase. Moreover, the best way to become great is to practice.

- Be sensitive to gender, political, religious and social groups in all of your written material and advertisements. You don't want to exclude anyone from potentially working with you.

Epilogue

One of the biggest elements of human nature is the need to belong to something bigger than ourselves. An MLM allows us an ongoing opportunity that encourages our participation and that of our friends.

Together we have reviewed the basics of building something bigger than ourselves. And the lessons we have learned are the tried-and-true handbook of building a wealthy business.

Wealth includes friends, family, long term relationships with associates, and those in our business support team. Together, we can celebrate free enterprise and the life many only dream of.

Without using these time-tested approaches, we have seen many independent business participants lost in the shuffle of day-to-day confusion. Turnover in this industry is a function of the inability of people to adhere to simple plans and implementation.

Failure comes when you ignore the counsel of a mentor, repeatedly miss weekly meetings, and fritter away precious time and energy on the internet instead of using it as a tool to promote your business.

It is easy in the face of failure to blame your business support team, spouse, neighbors, friends, cousins or dog, but the one place you must not forget to look is at yourself.

You yourself are responsible for your success, for your happiness, for your financial freedom. Don't allow yourself to be caught in the rut of blaming anyone else for your failures or lack of ambition.

If you apply the lessons you have learned and you use your abilities and potential to their highest, you will find happiness, fulfillment and success beyond measure.

I want to leave you with a few examples of what it means to be part of something bigger than yourself. Putting aside ego, think about any task that you wanted to accomplish but did not know exactly how. Think about the fears that you experienced and the hesitancy on your part. It is not easy to admit to those moments but they exist for all of us. Typically, we do one of two things:

First we walked away and decided not to tackle that challenge. This is easy, no possible pain, definitely no possible gain. Many of us chose this path. It is true you can't keep doing the same things and expect different results.

The second approach found us embracing the challenge, learning as much as we could during the growing process and then usually succeeding. Do we always succeed? No, that is not how life works. It is when we try something and are willing to fail that we have major breakthroughs as a direct result of our learning. We start to do different things and take different actions that empower us to succeed at a faster rate.

Life builds upon obstacles and as we tackle and overcome them, we learn and broaden our horizons. If you begin today, building your business, working through obstacles you will never wonder where life could have taken you, you will know for sure.
Take the basics of this business, couple them with the power of the internet, and you will find that leads, followers, retention rates and interest in your offer will expand geometrically.

Many organizations over the years have come and gone, and those that are still around are here because everybody teamed together their belief and support to keep the dream alive. This support system is coveted by other networking groups around the globe. So consider yourself lucky to be in the right place at the right time with the best opportunity this century will ever see. Now go out and be your best and the best is yours for the taking.

Glossary
Of computer & internet terms

BROWSER
A program that lets you display a file containing hypertext and graphic images. The browser also lets you navigate from one hypertext file to another via links using URLs.

CACHE
Memory holding recently accessed data designed to speed up subsequent access to the same data. The term cache is often applied to processor-memory access but can also be used to indicate a local copy of data internet accessible within a network.

CLIENT
A computer system or process that requests a service of another computer system or process --referred to as a server. For example, a workstation requesting the contents of a file from a file server is a client of the file server.

COOKIE
A handle, transaction ID or other token of agreement between cooperating programs.
An HTTP cookie is data sent by an HTTP server to a browser and then sent back by the browser each time that it accesses that server. Typically, an HTTP cookie is used to authenticate or identify a registered user of a web site without requiring an additional sign-in every time that site is accessed.

CONNECTION PROFILE
List of access telephone numbers dialed by your modem to connect to the internet. There are often several access telephone numbers available to an area.

DATAGRAM
A packet format with internet headers defined by the internet protocol. Datagrams are self-contained, independent entities carrying sufficient information to be routed from the source to the destination computer without relying on earlier exchanges between this source and destination computer and the transporting network. Datagrams are small and of a fixed size.

DATA PACKET
The basic unit of information exchange between computers engaged in data communications.

DIAL-UP ATTEMPTS
Maximum number of redials attempts.

DIAL-UP DELAY
Delay in seconds before making redial attempts.

DNS (Domain Name System)
Query service used on the Internet for translating hostnames into Internet addresses. DNS can be configured to use a sequence of name servers, based on the domains in the name being looked for, until a match is found.

DNS LIST
A short lst of DNS servers used for lookups. The list is used when your personal computer is acting like a mail server.

DNS TIME OUT
Time in seconds you program your computer to wait for valid DNS lookups.

DOMAIN
Refers to a group of computers whose hostnames share a common suffix, the domain name. Some common domains are:
.com = commercial / .edu = educational / .net = network
.gov = U.S. government / .mil = U.S. military
Most countries also have a domain:
.us = United States / .uk = United Kingdom / .au = Australia

DOMAIN HOST
The hosting company that supports your website.

DOMAIN NAME
Also known as your web address and usually starts with a (www.) followed by yourcompanyname.com.

EMAIL
The act of sending correspondence electronically.

EMAIL ADDRESS
The screen name you use to send or receive email.

E-NEWSLETTER
An official form of correspondence sent electronically for intended business purposes.

E-ADVERTISEMENT
An electronic advertisement sent or received through email or viewed on a website.

FTPSERVER
The name of the FTP server. FTP servers are used to upload and download files.

FILTER REGION
E-mail filtering by geographical location.

FILTERWORDS
E-mail filtering by keywords. E-mail addresses containing a keyword are filtered.

HOSTNAME
The unique name by which a computer is known on a network. The hostname is used to identify the computer in electronic mail, Usenet news, or other forms of electronic information exchange.

HTML (HyperText Markup Language)
The markup language with which World Wide Web documents are written. HTML lets you create hypertext links, fill-in forms and clickable images.

HTTP (HyperText Transfer Protocol)
An application-level protocol for distributed, hypermedia information systems. HTTP/1.0 is the version presently used. HTTP/1.1 is in pre-release stage.

HYPERMEDIA
An extension of hypertext that includes graphics sounds video and other kinds of data.

HYPERLINK
A web address added to an email or web page, that when clicked takes you directly to the website matching that address.

ISP (Internet Service Provider)
A provider of service such as America Online, Earthlink, MSN, Quixnet, or CompuServe through which you can access the internet.

IM (Instant Message)
This is a message sent to you in real time from another person on the internet. Conversations can be typed back and forth in an instant message much like the conversation that occurs in a telephone call.

INTERNIC (Internet Network Information Center)
A group funded by the National Science Foundation that maintains and distributes information about TCP/IP and the global Internet (e.g., documentation of work on the Internet, proposals for new or revised protocols and TCP/IP protocol standards), provides directory and database services, and provides registration services.

IP (Internet Protocol Address).
A unique 32-bit number specified as four 8-bit numbers called octets. The four octets are connected by periods. The numbers must be in the range 0-255. A sample IP address is 255.32.3.10.
This address is often assigned by a government agency called the DDN Network Information Center (NIC).

LAN (Local Access Network)
The access phone number is the telephone number dialed by your modem to connect to your internet service provider.

LOADING
The process a browser goes through to translate and bring up on your screen your web page from computer codes to text and pictures that are easy to read.

MAILLOG
A list that documents email transactions.

MESSAGE ATTACHMENT
This is a file to be attached to the message when sending e-mail or when posting to newsgroups.

MESSAGE BODY
This is the main message when sending e-mail or when posting to newsgroups.

MESSAGE ORGANIZATION
This will be the organization field when sending e-mail or when posting to newsgroups.

MESSAGE SUBJECT
The title or headline in the subject line of an email.

NETWORKING
The act of connecting two or more computers together for sharing files.

NEWSGROUP
Groups of people on the internet who join a chatroom live to discuss a topic of mutual interest.

NNTP DATLIST
Path to a newsgroup mail merge data file. Mail merge data files allow you to post highly customized articles.

NNTP SERVER
NNTP servers are used to send newsgroup postings.

PPP
Is a modem-based TCP/IP connection available through your local internet service provider.

POP SERVER
POP servers are used to receive e-mail.

PROTOCOL
A set of formal rules describing how to transmit data, especially across a network including the syntax of messages, the terminal-to-computer dialog, character sets, and sequencing of messages.

PROXY
An intermediary program that acts as both a server and a client for the purpose of making requests on behalf of other clients.

SCREENNAME
Also known as an email address and the name used to send or receive email or attachments electronically.

SERVER
An application program that accepts connections in order to service requests by sending back responses.

SIGNATURE
An automatic and electronic signature commonly found at the conclusion of an email or e-newsletter. A signature typically includes contact information for the sender.

SMTP SERVER
SMTP servers are used to send e-mail.

SPAM
Also known as bulk email. This is when you send an unsolicited mass mailing to people you do or do not know.

TCP/IP (Transmission Control Protocol / Internet Protocol) is a communications format for transferring data on a network. You can use if it is available on your computer instead of a modem to connect to your local internet service provider. And it is often faster than the usual modem-based connection process.

TRANSIT NETWORK
A network that passes traffic between other networks in addition to carrying traffic for its own hosts. It must have paths to at least two other networks.

URL (Uniform Resource Locator)
is the global address of documents and other resources on the World Wide Web.

WWW - (World Wide Web)
A universal library that hosts millions of web pages, articles, and web sites.

WEB SITE
A site location on the World Wide Web. Each site contains a home page, which is the first document users see when going to the site. The site might also contain additional pages of text and is owned usually by an individual or company.

WEBPAGE - A document on the World Wide Web. Every page is identified by a unique URL or Web address.

Resources

Federal Trade Commission
CRC-240
Washington, D.C. 20580
Phone: 1-877-FTC-HELP (382-4357)
www.ftc.gov

The National Fraud Information Center
PO Box 65868
Washington, DC 20035
800-876-7060
www.fraud.org

The Direct Selling Association
1666 K Street, NW, Suite 1010
Washington DC 20006-2808
(202) 293-5760
Fax: (202) 463-4569
www.dsa.org

American City Business Journals
To locate a Business Journal in your area with listings to community
meetings, chamber of commerce activities, Toastmasters clubs and
more.
American City Business Journals
120 West Morehead Street
Charlotte NC 28202
Phone: 704-973-1000 Fax: 704-973-1001
www.bizjournals.com

Toastmasters International
For a link to a Toastmaster club near you.
Toastmasters International
PO Box 9052
Mission Viejo, CA 92690
www.Toastmasters.org

www.WordsofWellness.com - List of daily motivational tips to keep you at your best while in business for yourself.

www.webopedia.com - The only online dictionary and search engine you need for computer and Internet technology.

www.zdtv.com
Find an Internet Service Provider with the List, a buyer's guide to internet service providers updated daily by ZDTV. You can check out their web site at.
Internet service providers are gateways to the Web and number over 7,500 in the United States alone. Search by area code, country code, United States or Canada, and a list of companies in your area pop up. The INTERNET SERVICE PROVIDER Profiles show useful information, like service area, software, access speed, and fees.

The Dish Network
A company that provides digital satellite dishes and receivers with built in Web TV capabilities called a "DishPlayer". This allows you to access entertainment programming as well as internet access and web surfing.
DISH Network
P.O. Box 33577
Northglenn, CO 80233
1-800-333-DISH
WWW.DishNetwork.com

WebTV

The original TV/internet system that allows you to go web surfing and connect internet access through your home television.
WebTV Networks, Inc.
1250 Charleston Road
Mountain View, CA 94043
1.800.GO.WEBTV or 1.800.469.3288.
www.webtv.com

United States Post Office

Contact your local post office about bulk mail permits preprinted bulk mailing, post office box rental, inexpensive overnight delivery, two-three day priority delivery.
Look up their web site for a post office near you.
www.usps.gov

www.PostMasterDirect.com

Target your e-newsletters and e-advertisements with 100% OPT-IN email marketing! Every list owned, managed or brokered by Post-MasterDirect.com® is 100% opt-in. This means that every name on their lists belongs to an Internet user who has gone to their site or sites of their affiliates and voluntarily signed up to receive commercial email about topics of interest. They host over 9,000 opt-in lists and over 3 million unique names to choose from! Only .10 to .30 cents a name, (a low $400 minimum order) includes list rental, email distribution and merge/purge! With this option you don't need any fancy mailing software, you simply pay a fee and PostMasterDirect.com® processes your email.

Prices are about the same you would pay through the regular postal service, only you receive your responses much quicker. It is like express mail advertising at regular or discounted bulk mailing rates.

Marketers that have used them have generated response rates as high as 5 to 15 percent which is unheard of in the direct mail industry. They are breaking new ground in e-commerce and have been touted as the experts leading the field by The New York Times, The Wall Street Journal, Business Week, DM News, Advertising Age and other leading publications.

Check them out at www.PostMasterDirect.com®

PostMasterDirect.Com®

379 West Broadway, Suite 202

New York, NY,10012

212-625-1370

www.cyberatlas.com for the latest up to the minute internet statistics and market research to find out what trends are raking in the dough through e-commerce.

Learn about traffic patterns to web sites, who is interested in what, Tips on how companies can maximize their advertising dollar.

Sign up for their free weekly electronic newsletter.

Sign up or free e-newsletters in the following categories:

at http://e-newsletters.internet.com

- Small business owners
- E-Commerce
- Systems Administrator
- HTML
- Web Design and Promotion
- Web Site Development
- Web Site Tracking
- Web Site Tracking
- Web Marketing
- Web Investing
- IT Professionals
- Web Site Security
- Web Technology
- Java
- Webmaster
- Web Designers
- Web Advertising
- Web Site Statistics
- Finance-Investing
- Web Software

- Internet Shoppers
- Internet ISP Business
- Web Hosting Services

- Internet Businesses
- ISP Business

Track Your Business support team

Network-marketing software enables you to keep track of your accounts, your database, and your profits. Here are four programs that won't eat into your revenue. And the best part is you can download a free trial version of these programs from the company web sites so you can determine which one is best for your needs.

MLM Easy Money

And because you can never be too ambitious, both versions allow you to juggle as many as three separate network-marketing companies at a time.

When you open the program, the helpful setup wizard walks you through inputting your company information and setting up such basics as sales-tax and shipping calculations.

The income and expenses features track your accounting records, whether you earn money from sales commissions, through bonuses, or by any other means. MLM Easy Money keeps track of all the items you purchase for resale, lets you view your on-site inventory, and generates a purchase summary. The Professional edition offers checkbook and credit card registers automatic invoicing and back-logging, reports of sales by customer, group e-mail broadcasting, and more.

Kynetics Software
268 Ruby Avenue
San Carlos, CA 94070
1-877.632.9988 (toll free)
www.kynetics.com

Standard Edition $59.95
Professional Edition $89.95

MLM Office

Resembles your favorite Windows-based contact manager, but it adds a few extra touches, including fields for the name of the contact's sponsor. This program also helps you manage your organization; and for a quick overview of everyone in your group, you can print a support team report. For staying in touch, the automated e-mail lets you send and receive e-mail messages from within the program. What about inventory, ordering, and payment tracking? It's all there in MLM Office, and you can print a packing slip with a single mouse click.

Productivity Systems   Standard Edition $39.95
www.prodsysinc.com/mlmoffice

MLMPRO

MLMPro offers more than 200 templates for different network-marketing companies, so you can follow their strategies for setting up and maintaining your business support team, database, to-do list, and more. To keep in touch with your business support team, you can send or receive e-mail from within MLMPro, provided you have an ISP account; it won't work with such commercial online services as America Online and Prodigy. But unlike other programs that include inventory and order tracking, MLMPro concentrates on contact management.

InTouch Communications   Standard Edition $99.95
1-604-469-9662
www.mlmpro.com

Networker 2.2
Networker 2.2 is the perfect software for the beginning network marketer. Its tutorial walks you through setting up your network-marketing information; imports your names, addresses, and phone numbers from your old manager; and links with your telephone, so all you need to do is double-click on someone's name, and your phone starts dialing.

How do you keep track of everyone you meet? The Prospect List Expert uses memory joggers to help you create a list prospects you can contact today.
Call up the Prospect List Expert; then enter in your contact information, and assign one of three different apple icons to each name.

Along with an events calendar complete with alarms that you can set to remind you of important dates (such as birthdays and anniversaries), Networker lets you send names from its Prospect List to your Call List for that day's phone calls.

MLMSoft Corp.   Standard Edition $69.00
888-656-7638
www.mlmsoft.com

E-newsletter Software / Mailloop
Mailloop is the complete internet email, bulk email, newsletter server, web form processor, customer database, newsgroup poster, and autoresponder solution. Instead of doing all your daily tasks manually this software will do it for you? Spend your time marketing and growing your business, not doing daily chores, email, etc. It even has a built-in scheduler so it will turn itself on and do the tasks whenever you ask it to! And it all runs from our home PC.

It is only available online and must be downloaded.
Check www.mailloop.com for system requirements new features.

Standard Edition $399.00

Microsoft Office

Here you can find multimedia demos, see the latest Office features in action. Get upgrades, product details along with product demos, read about Office programs, system requirements, trial software, and why to upgrade. From this website, you can also read reviews; see what awards have been given, and customize your office choices based on your computing needs.

Prices vary and are all updated online along with purchasing options and support.

www.microsoft.com/office

Recommended Reading

100 Ways to Motivate Yourself by Steve Chandler, (1996) ISBN:1564142493, Career Press US Dollars $15.99

Advertising on the Internet by Robbin Lee Zeff, Brad Aronson, Bradley Aronson (1997) ISBN:047118330X, John Wiley & Sons, US Dollars $19.00

Being the Best You Can Be in MLM by John *Kalench* (1990) ISBN:096294470X, Millionaires in Motion, Incorporated, US Dollars $14.95.

Building a Mail Order Business: A Complete Manual for Success (4th Ed) by William A. Cohen (1996) John Wiley & Sons; ISBN: 0471109460 US Dollars $42.95

Charisma by Tony Alessandra 1998, ISBN:0446520497, Warner Books, Incorporated, US Dollars $23.50.

Cybertalk That Sells by Herschell Gordon Lewis; Jamie Murphy, (1998) ISBN:0809229234,
N T C/Contemporary Publishing Company, US Dollars $14.95.

Dig Your Well Before You're Thirsty by Harvey Mackay (1999) ISBN:0385485468, Doubleday, US Dollars $14.95.

Grow Rich with Peace of Mind by Napoleon Hill (1988) ISBN:0449215253, Fawcett Book Group, US Dollars $5.95.

How to Get Anything You Want by Nido R. Qubein (1998) ISBN:0939975157, Executive Press, US Dollars $29.95.

How to Get Rich in Mail Order by Melvin Powers (1981) ISBN:0879803738, Wilshire Book Co; US Dollars $20.00.

Power of the Plus Factor by Norman Vincent Peale (1996) ISBN:0449912094, Fawcett Book Group, US Dollars $10.00.

Reaching Your Potential by Norman Vincent Peale (1997) ISBN:0517185423, Random House Value Publishing, Incorporated, US Dollars $6.99.

Street-Smart Network Marketing by Robert *Butwin* (1997) ISBN:0761510001, Prima Publishing, US Dollars $14.00.

Success Through a Positive Mental Attitude by Napoleon Hill (1991) ISBN:0671743228, Pocket Books, US Dollars $6.99

The Network Marketer's Guide to Success by Jeffrey Babener; David Stewart (1990) ISBN:0962805505, Forum for Network Marketing, The, US Dollars $24.95.

Think & Grow Rich by Napoleon Hill (1987) ISBN: 0449214923, Fawcett Book Group, US Dollars $5.99.

Tongue Fu! Sam Horn (1996) ISBN:0312140541, Saint Martin's Press, Incorporated, US Dollars $22.95.

Sources

Duncan Maxwell Anderson, *Unstoppable Crusade*: John Milton Fogg Set Out to Celebrate a Way of Life Where People Who Help one Another Get Nicer and Richer., Success, Oct 1997 v44 n8 p84(2).

Doug Beizer, *Return to Sender,* PC Magazine, March 10, 1998 v17 n5 p40(1).

Dana Blankenhorn, *E-mail Flexes Its Marketing Muscle,* Business Marketing, July 1997 v82 n6 p28(1).

Harriet B. Braiker, *The Power of Self-talk,* Psychology Today, Dec 1989 v23 n12 p23(5).

Bob Burg, *Ten Tips for Effective Networking,* The National Public Accountant, June 1991 v36 n6 p44(1).

James Champy, *E-Commerce Winners and Losers,* Sales & Marketing Management, July 1999 v151 i7 p32.

James Champy, *The Cyber-Future is Now,* Sales & Marketing Management, Sept 1997 v149 n9 p28(2).

Sacha Cohen, *Got Email?,* Training & Development, Oct 1997 v51 n10 p21(3).

Barb Cole-Gomolski, *E-mail's Double-Edged Sword,* Computerworld, Feb 23, 1998 v32 n8 p28(1).

Mike Dries, *E-mail Etiquette Traps Even Conscientious in Net,* Sacramento Business Journal, Sep 5, 1997 v14 n25 p20(1).

Sean M. Dugan, *The State of I-Commerce,* InfoWorld, July 19, 1999 v21 i29 p36.

Ron Ellsmore, *Second Thoughts about Confidence,* American Salesman, Dec 1996 v41 n12 p16(4).

Barry Evans, *Speed Bumps on the Information Super Highway,* Petersen's Photographic, August 1999 v28 i4 p96(1).

Martin Focazio, *How Effective is Your E-mail?,* Getting Results, July 1997 v42 n7 p4(1).

Susan Greco, *The Buddy System,* Inc., Oct 22, 1996 v18 n15 p52(6).

Richard Grossman, *The Confidence Game,* Health, April 1984 v16 p10(1).

Pat Haas, *The First Door,* American Salesman, Oct 1990 v35 n10 p6(3).

Henry R. Hoke, *E-mail Overload,* Direct Marketing, Feb 1998 v60 n10 p80(1).

Rich Karlgaard, *The Lessons of Email Deceit,* Forbes, Oct 6, 1997 v160 n7 pS13(1).

Bill Kelley, *How to Make Friends and Sell to People,* Sales & Marketing Management, August 1989 v141 n9 p40(3).

Paul Klebnikov, *The Power of Positive Inspiration.*, Forbes, Dec 9, 1991 v148 n13 p244

David S. Klein, *The Eight-fold Path to E-commerce*, Business Marketing, Nov 1997 v82 n10 p17(1).

Herschell Gordon Lewis, *A Small Point of Personal Privilege*, Direct Marketing, Nov 1997 v60 n7 p38(2).

Eric Lundquist, *Your Best Contribution to Your E-business is...*,PC Week, July 26, 1999 v16 i30 p106.

G.A. Marken, *PR E-mail ... Overused, Abused and Invaluable*, Public Relations Quarterly, Winter 1997 v42 n4 p20(3).

Rodman Marymor and Jeffrey Rasco, *Push Technology Can Be Too Pushy*, Meetings & Conventions, Dec 1997 v32 n13 p36(1)

Mike McCaffrey, *Six Steps to Getting What You Want in Life*, American Salesman, August 1996 v41 n8 p6(2).

Melonee McKinney, *Mass Retailers Look at Internet Options*, Daily News Record, July 12, 1999 p16.

Michael J. Miller, *Are You Really Safe Online?*, PC Magazine, Sept 1, 1999 v18 i15 p4.
Megan Monson, *The Subtle Art of Netiquette*, Oregon Business, July 1997 v20 n7 p59(2).

James Morrow, *Promote Yourself!*, Success, Jan 1999 v46 i1 p76(1).

Hallie Mummert, *New List Rules*, Target Marketing, August 1996 v19 n8 p32(3).

184

Ted Pollock, *How to be Totally Sure of Yourself*, American Salesman, Nov 1991 v36 n11 p21(6).

Phil Rafter, *Keep up With Downlines*, Success, April 1999 v46 i4 p90(1).

Matthew Reed, *E-commerce: An Era of Confusion.*, Marketing, June 17, 1999 p27(2).

Rosalind Resnick, *Dos & Don'ts of E-mail Marketing*, Target Marketing, Jan 1998 v21 n1 pS8(1).

Sana Reynolds, *Composing Effective E-mail Messages*, Communication World, July 15, 1997 v14 n7 p8(2).

Ronaleen R. Roha, *The Ups and Downs of "Downlines."*, Kiplinger's Personal Finance Magazine, Nov 1991 v45 n11 p63(6).

Uma Sackett (Interview with Randy Gage), *Get Rich Quick: is There Such Thing as a Free Lunch?* Success, March 1998 v45 n3 p66(2).

Michael Schrage, *What Makes E-mail Worth Forwarding?*, Computerworld, Jan 19, 1998 v32 n3 p37(1).

Dylan Tweney, *Net Prophet*, InfoWorld, July 12, 1999 v21 i28 p52.

Michael Vizard, *E-commerce Goes Multilingual*, InfoWorld, July 19, 1999 v21 i29 p16.

Eric Ward, *How to Make The Most of E-mail Releases*, Business Marketing, May 1997 v82 n4 pM3(2).

Mark B. Yarnell, *Recruiting the Stars: Anatomy of an MLM Success.* Success, Jan-Feb 1994 v41 n1 p12(1).

Kristine Ziwica, *ABCD...MLM.*, Success, May 1999 v46 i5 p78(1)

Index

188

www.ingramcontent.com/pod-product-compliance
Lightning Source LLC
Chambersburg PA
CBHW020314220326
41519CB00066B/522